Boomers 3.0

Boomers 3.0

Marketing to Baby Boomers in Their Third Act of Life

Lawrence R. Samuel

PRAEGER™

An Imprint of ABC-CLIO, LLC

Santa Barbara, California • Denver, Colorado

Library of Congress Cataloging-in-Publication Data

Names: Samuel, Lawrence R., author.
Title: Boomers 3.0 : marketing to baby boomers in their third act of life / Lawrence R. Samuel.
Description: Santa Barbara : Praeger, [2017] | Includes bibliographical references and index.
Identifiers: LCCN 2017013909 (print) | LCCN 2017028966 (ebook) | ISBN 9781440857232 (ebook) | ISBN 9781440857225 (alk. paper)
Subjects: LCSH: Baby boom generation—United States—History. | Baby boom generation—Retirement—United States. | Baby boom generation—United States—Social conditions—21th century. | Health attitudes—United States.
Classification: LCC HN59.2 (ebook) | LCC HN59.2 .S256 2017 (print) | DDC 305.2—dc23
LC record available at https://lccn.loc.gov/2017013909

ISBN: 978-1-4408-5722-5
EISBN: 978-1-4408-5723-2

21 20 19 18 17   1 2 3 4 5

This book is also available as an eBook.

Praeger
An Imprint of ABC-CLIO, LLC

ABC-CLIO, LLC
130 Cremona Drive, P.O. Box 1911
Santa Barbara, California 93116-1911
www.abc-clio.com

This book is printed on acid-free paper ∞

Manufactured in the United States of America

Contents

Preface

First things first: this is not your ordinary business book. This is a book about baby boomers, and how to translate that knowledge into marketing opportunities that resonate with that very large, very wealthy group of consumers who were born between 1946 and 1964. Only by knowing the driving passions and operative values of any particular group of consumers can an organization develop compelling marketing opportunities, an approach that, I firmly believe, has gained considerable currency in recent years but is still not fully appreciated by many companies. Cultural fluency is the key to the marketplace, my experience tells me, with only a holistic, 360-degree understanding of consumers capable of revealing the kind of innovative ideas that lead to breakthrough success.

All that said, there is plenty of information here that draws from the world of business, specifically which marketers are most effectively tapping into the cultural DNA of boomers, how they are doing that, and what we can learn from it. I show how organizations of all sizes and in all industries and product categories can create meaningful relationships with baby boomers in their third act of life based on how the group is spending our two principal resources: time and money. Rather than describe what boomers say, think, or say they think—the focus of almost all market research—I am solely interested in what they are actually doing. Taking a behavioral versus attitudinal approach is the only means of cracking the code of any target market, and the reason why dozens of Fortune 500 companies and their ad agencies have hired me as a consultant.

The second thing to know about this book is that it is unapologetically pro-boomer. I was born in the sweet spot of the birth spike of the generation that came to be known as baby boomers because of their high numbers and have some personal experience with all of the seminal moments (most notably duck-and-cover drills, the Beatles' appearance on *The Ed Sullivan Show*, the assassinations of JFK, MLK, and RFK, the first moon landing, and the era's final hurrah, Woodstock) that are commonly associated with the group. This historical legacy has become so familiar that it seems like to some as a movie that one has watched too many times, part of the reason for the widespread antipathy directed at the group. Baby boomer bashing has long been in vogue, of course, with the "me generation" earning its selfish reputation in the hedonistic 1970s and its greed-is-good image in the materialistic 1980s.

Recently, however, criticism directed toward boomers has become especially nasty, a by-product of the negative feelings many younger people have about older people in general. Boomers comprise "a bloated pile of historical ego and overinflated cultural self-importance," wrote Jason Notte in thestreet.com in 2014, a typical example of the tendency among some Gen Xers (now in their mid-thirties to early fifties) and millennials (often defined as 18- to 34-year-olds) to dismiss older Americans' unsurpassed contributions to society that continue to this day. In a nutshell, according to the many boomer haters (just Google "baby boomers" if you have any doubt about this), the generation deserves principal blame for most if not all of the biggest problems of the country and the world. "Boomers soaked up a lot of economic opportunity without bothering to preserve much for the generations to come," posited Jim Tankersley, a writer for the *Washington Post*, the following year, thinking that their main legacy was having "burned a lot of cheap fossil fuels and filling the atmosphere with heat-trapping gases."

If boomers' collective past has been portrayed as either much ado about nothing or environmentally disastrous, according to such critics, their future is nothing short of apocalyptic. Because of their numbers and greedy tendencies, this theory goes (backed up by many economists), boomers will wreck the American economy and health care system as they age, with millennials having to pick up the tab. Some go even further by saying it's due time boomers just got out of the way and allow younger generations to make their own mark in society, a classic case of ageism that has no place in American society. Putting older people on an ice flow to let them float away, as the (factually false) Eskimo legend goes, would seem to suit such boomer haters just fine. Memo to such historically challenged folks: boomers have no interest in going gently into that good night (or even to a retirement community in Florida), so we all should get used to the idea of having them around for at least the next couple of decades. This is actually a very good thing, this book shows, as some of boomers' greatest contributions to society lie ahead. Millennials no doubt have a great future ahead of them, and my wish is that they achieve an equally great set of things in their own lifetimes.

Often overlooked in such hostile accusations and misinformed predictions are the startling array of achievements baby boomers have realized since the first one was born a little over 70 years ago. In my nonbusiness life, I am a cultural historian and have written many books in which boomers have served as the protagonists of the 20th century. Growing up in the Cold War, when it was commonly believed that the world could blow up at any point, gave boomers a sense of urgency to accomplish great things, many of which they actually did. Boomers fought bravely in the Vietnam War, led a cultural revolution grounded in the noble ideas of peace and equality, and then embarked on careers that propelled this nation to become the most powerful and wealthiest in civilization. Along the way, they popularized if not downright invented things like rock 'n' roll, the computer, and the Internet, all the while giving more money away to worthy causes than any previous generation. Boomers were undeniably fortunate to have come of age during the latter half of the amazing "American Century"; they greatly benefited from the incredible scientific and technological strides made in the postwar years, and happened to be in the right place at the right time when the nation was ready to reinvent itself in the late 1960s. Launching and continuing their careers in the economically advantageous 1980s and 1990s was also good timing, and the steadily upward tick of the stock market and escalation of real estate prices over the last decade and a half has only added to the net worth of many boomers.

While this book is in some sense a celebration of boomer culture and rejoinder against the rising tide of vitriol directed at the group, I recognize the generation has not fully lived up to its potential. Many have abused their physical selves in a manner to make them as a group less healthy than they could and perhaps should have been at an advanced age given their obsession with "naturalness" when young. ("I would have treated my body better had I known I would have lived this long" is a commonly heard refrain.) As well, some of boomers' preferences in popular culture over the years were questionable at best (I personally apologize for disco and the urban cowboy craze of the late 1970s and early 1980s), and they undeniably took conspicuous consumption to an entirely new level. More recently, boomers have failed to form any kind of significant coalition to fight virulent ageism, instead futilely trying to hang on to the remnants of their rapidly fading youth. Given their roots in social activism, this is a lost opportunity, and I urge my fellow boomers to take on the cause in their third act of life in a way that they combated racial and gender prejudice and an unjust war in their first and second acts.

Introduction

Really? A book about marketing to boomers? As the most consumptive generation in history, do boomers even need to be marketed to?

In a word, yes. *Boomers 3.0: Marketing to Baby Boomers in Their Third Act of Life* shows how to market to baby boomers from a cultural perspective, filling a very large gap in the universe of business books. "Boomers 3.0" is a reference to the third (and final) version of boomers' lives, a period of time that has already begun and will extend to the 2040s. The first version of boomers lives' (Boomers 1.0) comprised their childhood and young adulthood from the 1950s to the 1970s. The second version (Boomers 2.0) encompassed their middle adulthood from the 1980s through the 2000s. *Boomers 3.0* thus addresses baby boomers' later adulthood that will continue for the next two to three decades. Boomers' third act of life will be different from their first and second, I propose, meaning organizations should take a different approach to marketing to them than in the past. Creating meaningful relationships with baby boomers in their third act of life should be a priority for all kinds of businesses, something that demands a new kind of thinking and an alternative set of tools. This book offers a way to contextualize business objectives within a culturally based, forward-thinking framework that fully leverages what is perhaps the biggest story of our time and place.

Doing so will be well worth the effort. A solid case can be made that the graying of America or age wave is the most significant socioeconomic trend today, as 65 million (of the original 76 million) boomers (who in 2017 range in age from 53 to 71) head into their senior years *en masse*.

Nearly 10,000 boomers are turning 65 everyday, an unprecedented demographic tsunami. In 2029, the year when the last boomer will have turned 65, there will still be over 61 million boomers, according to the Census Bureau, about 17.2 percent of the projected population of the United States.[1] Virtually all arenas of life in the United States will be affected by this mass migration into seniority. Much concern revolves around boomers' entitlements and their future health care needs, with a generational war predicted to be fought with millennials over taxpayer resources. While this apocalyptic scenario is open to debate (I think the aging of boomers will actually help the economy and society at large by creating millions of much-needed jobs), there is no doubt that the aging of what was the largest generation in history (until the millennials came around) will have a profound social, economic, and political impact on America and Americans.

The aging of America also presents major implications for businesses in virtually all industries and product categories. Boomers are still the key to the marketplace despite marketers' (and America's) obsession with youth, much in part to their collective wealth and propensity to consume. As a group, boomers are going to have the highest net worth in the United States until at least 2030, according to the Deloitte Center for Financial Services, with their portion of total assets less liabilities to reach a high of 50 percent by 2020. By 2030, boomers' net household wealth is forecast to be 44.5 percent, still an impressive number that marketers will have to take into account when choosing whom to target with products and services.[2]

Likewise, boomers' buyer power is and will remain huge. While boomers represent about a quarter of the nation's population, they currently hold 70 percent of disposable income, according to a report by Nielsen and BoomAgers. Boomers are buying about half of total consumer-packaged goods (CPGs) and dominate purchases in 119 of 123 CPG categories, more reason why marketers should not think the group's best consumer days are behind them.[3]

In fact, when compared with boomers, millennials are just not very good consumers, at least not yet. For better or worse, depending on one's view of consumerism in general, millennials have yet to latch onto the kind of debt-driven materialism boomers are famous for by not actively pursuing the two big-ticket items of cars and real estate. As well, 75 percent of millennials possess the financial resources to purchase only those things that they essentially must have versus what they desire, the ad agency and consultancy BoomAgers and the Natural Marketing Institute reported in 2015, with a whopping 45 percent of that generation underemployed and 23 percent carrying at least some debt from their college days. Most millennials are not going to receive their biggest paychecks before 2030, more reason that marketers should make a concerted effort to target boomers.[4]

To that point, widely held stereotypes of older consumers are just untrue. Most companies no doubt want to market to boomers because of their discretionary dollars and sheer numbers, but now may no longer know how to, thinking perhaps that older consumers are interested only in products and services for the aged. Research shows that most boomers are not interested in radically downsizing, however, and are open as ever to new brand experiences. As "professional" consumers their whole lives, boomers will keep spending money until they go off to the big Woodstock in the sky, making it a mistake for marketers to ignore them in their later years. Boomers "respect those brands that represent them faithfully while appealing to their values and ambitions at this stage of their lives," noted Peter Hubbell, author of *The Old Rush* and *Getting Better with Age*, correctly thinking an "age-inclusive" approach is in marketers' best interests.[5]

Boomers 3.0 rests on the assumption that baby boomers (or any other generation or socially constructed group) are a moving target. They may be basically the same people inside, but boomers are typically living different kinds of lives and seeing the world differently in their third act than they were and did in their first and second. This implies that new, innovative techniques are required to approach them as consumers. Likewise, boomers have been aggressively marketed to for about a half century now, this too suggesting that an alternative set of tools be used to effectively reach them as consumers. This book draws on the same kind of culture-based methodology I have used as a consultant to Fortune 500 companies and major advertising agencies for clients across a wide variety of industries and categories, including Anheuser Busch, Baskin-Robbins, Chase, Conde Nast, General Mills, Hasbro, John Hancock, Liberty Mutual, L.L. Bean, J.P. Morgan, and Whirlpool.

Bypassing a traditional marketing model for one that offers organizations the opportunity to create meaningful relationships with older but still very active consumers thus makes a lot of sense. With its cultural orientation and anthropological approach, *Boomers 3.0* is quite literally not business-as-usual, a good thing given the need to stand out in today's crowded marketplace and frenetic media environment. The net is greater cultural context for any organization's business planning and/or account planning process and the ideal platform for strategic planning, new product development, brand positioning, advertising, promotion, public relations, and social media. Although marketing and advertising people represent the book's sweet spot, free agent entrepreneurs to CEOs of large companies should find it useful in learning how to translate boomer culture into actionable and profitable results. Many managers are experts at running their respective businesses but freely admit they are less than culturally informed and have little idea how to convert market intelligence into implementable ideas. Small business owners and human resource people should also find the book helpful by gaining a better understanding of how to manage (and hopefully hire) boomer employees.

While no one can definitively say how boomers' third act of life will play out, it is safe to say that it will be quite different from their first and second. Boomers 1.0 was mostly about education and fun and 2.0 much about work and family, but there is no such overarching, defining narrative, at least yet, for 3.0. Powerful social, economic, and political forces that will shape boomers' future offer clues to their defining values, however. If the cultural revolution of the 1960s-1970s (the latter part of version 1.0) led to values like rebellion and hedonism and the neo-conservatism of the 1980s-2000s (version 2.0) was the foundation for materialism and domesticity, the multiculturalism and globalism of the 2010s-2040s (version 3.0) will no doubt be a catalyst for values related to activism and community.

However the future plays out, there is no getting around the fact that many boomers currently view aging as an inconvenient truth, a surprising and annoying fact of life. "How and when did I get old, or at least start appearing old to others?" boomers are asking themselves, with no easy answers forthcoming. This book shows that the distressing changes to one's body are often countered by an evolution of mind and spirit, however, with the third act of life typically a period of intellectual growth, accelerated creativity, emotional contentedness, and a desire to take on new challenges. More good news is the likelihood that many boomers will join forces and become a powerful social, economic, and political coalition, and will use their new power to fight for equal rights and their entitlements. Some of boomers' countercultural dream of creating a better world will thus ironically be achieved in their third act, with their final hurrah to be heavily defined by giving back and leaving some form of legacy to benefit society.

Consistent with a deep dive into the cultural dynamics of a very large, very diverse group of people, *Boomers 3.0* covers a lot of ground, including the arts; education; health care; home; online culture; retail; relationships and sexuality; spirituality; sports and recreation; travel; and work. Certain key themes run through the book, the most important being that baby boomers are not done yet. The "greatest generation" survived the Depression and saved the American Way of Life in World War II, but boomers are now reinventing the concept of older age—a historic achievement in itself. For the past century in the United States, the post-employment stage of life was viewed as a kind of epilogue to the main body of work. There were exceptions, of course, but people older than 65 were generally considered no longer active, productive, and contributing members of society. The passage of Social Security in the 1930s and Medicare in the 1960s were of tremendous benefit, but made older Americans appear like dependents, and further marginalized them from the rest of the "useful" population. Boomers are changing that perception, a cultural pivot point that will perhaps serve as their greatest legacy.

A big part of the rethinking of what constitutes "oldness" is the decreasing significance of biologically defined age. There is a greater understanding that one doesn't go to bed one night "young" and wake up the following morning "old" just because it happens to be your 50th, 60th, or 70th birthday, making such milestones increasingly less important. The virtual disappearance of mandatory retirement (usually at age 65) has also made one's age not the defining marker it used to be. The great variation in older people's physical and cognitive condition—a 70-year-old can be fit as a fiddle or a total wreck—is additional reason to no longer view biological age as a particularly reliable measure of who a person actually is.

Boomers' recasting of what used to be considered "old age" or one's "senior years" carries enormous cultural freight. By continuing to work and live active lives for as long as physically and mentally possible, boomers are blurring the lines between middle age and older age, in the process making the final phase of life not just a postscript to one's productive years. For the next couple of decades, anyway, the word "boomers" may even come to serve as the defining term of people who are in their mid-fifties or older, an interesting possibility. No one was ever really comfortable with the terminology associated with older people ("seniors," "matures," "elderly," and newly politically correct labels such as "seasoned citizens," "wellderly," or "superadults"), making such a scenario to me an attractive one.

The possible end of old age as we know it also poses major consequences for boomers' role as consumers. Should organizations even continue to think in terms of a market segment made up of "old" people? Will such a market continue to exist given boomers' determination not to look, act, or think "old"? I think not, and argue that organizations should no longer view older people as a specific demographic based on age. Rather, as this book makes plain, marketers should see boomers as that same generation of people who now happen to be moving into their third act of life and present their brands to them based on the driving values and passions outlined here.

Boomers famously rejected many of their parents' expectations since they were teenagers, of course, so it should not be too surprising that they are discarding that generation's model of older age for something else. Rather than view retirement as the last leg of their journey and a reward for a lifetime of hard work, boomers have a desire to learn and try new things, express their creativity, reconnect with people and form new, meaningful relationships, and give back by sharing time, money, and life lessons with others. Overall there is an urge to improve or refine themselves in their third act of life, with a conscious or unconscious striving for wisdom or self-actualization. Boomers are not the first generation to view later life as ideally a holistic experience that incorporates mind, body, and spirit, making this too a defining feature of their third act.

While boomers are clearly future-focused, that is, thinking about and planning for what may come next, the lens through which they view life is naturally shaped by the past. This makes perfect sense, as six decades or so of life is a lot of material to carry around in one's brain. Marketers tend to go overboard in drawing on the past when targeting boomers, however, too often treating them as walking repositories of memories. Boomers may very well have a storied past, both individually and collectively, but are just as likely as young people to be looking forward rather than backward. Again, one isn't young and then suddenly "old," as aging is a gradual process in which physical and cognitive changes take place over the course of many years. Likewise, seeing older age as a separate phase of life that follows the "real" one is a big mistake; boomers tend to think of themselves as essentially the same people they were when they were 20 or 30, although many research studies have shown that life experience has given them the ability to see things from a longer, broader perspective.

All of these insights serve as the backdrop for the scope and content of this book. Via its 10 chapters, *Boomers 3.0* describes the supporting framework or "pillars" of baby boomer culture, reflecting the core values of middle class+, cognitively healthy boomers in their third act of life (roughly age 55–80). The book presents what I believe to be are the building blocks of boomer identity, both now and for the foreseeable future. The goal is to provide a snapshot of the individual and collective DNA that guides boomers' attitudes and behavior in order to have a better sense of how they are likely to spend their time and money in the future.

For marketers, each chapter of *Boomers 3.0* represents a territory to stake and mine with products, services, and communications. Each chapter can stand on its own, but they occasionally overlap, as no individual, much less a group of 65 million people, can be sliced and diced into neatly divided pieces. In fact, places where the content does cross over, such as volunteerism or AARP, are especially opportunistic, as they make up a bigger or stronger component of boomer DNA. Within each chapter are six "passion points"—things and experiences that resonate on a visceral level with boomers and represent their behavioral paper trail. Each passion point concludes with an Opportunity statement designed to serve as a jumping off point for marketers to explore based on their unique set of business initiatives and goals. Enjoy the ride!

ONE

Fountain of Youth

A lot of people can't stand touring but to me it's like breathing.

Bob Dylan

Dylan is very much living up to his words. The 75-year-old singer-songwriter and Nobel Prize winner was an icon of baby boomer culture in the 1960s (although he was actually not one himself), and to this day he embodies the spirit of the generation who will always remain at some level forever young. Dylan is constantly on the road, not about to retire to his house in Malibu to stare out into the ocean and remember better days. While the man's body has aged, he is doing exactly the same thing as he did while JFK was president, an amazing achievement by any measure.

While Bob Dylan is no doubt a remarkable specimen (other still active 70-something musicians include Paul McCartney, Rod Stewart, Tina Turner, Aretha Franklin, Neil Diamond, Paul Simon, and members of the Rolling Stones), many members of the generation he inspired are displaying clear signs of perpetual youth. Although one's body may not have got the memo, youth is not something that necessarily goes away at age 20, 30, or any other chronological measure. Rather, youthfulness is an idea that anyone, regardless of his or her age, can subscribe to as part of an approach to or philosophy of life. This is especially true for boomers, who broke away from their parents' generation by adopting a lifestyle and political orientation that immediately became associated with youthful values. Well after the counterculture, many boomers held onto their determination to remain in some way "forever young," and to this very day are committed as ever to thinking, acting, and appearing young. Some millennials perhaps wish their parents' generation would get out of the way and move on to greener pastures (just as boomers wished), but this simply isn't going to happen.

Much of the commentary about the aging of boomers understandably revolves around the difference between them and the "greatest generation." The defining moments in boomers' parents' generation was the Depression, World War II, and postwar conformity—events or cultural phenomena that perhaps made them old before their time. Boomers' defining moments were events or cultural phenomena like Woodstock, protests against the Vietnam War, and the counterculture—things that one could say are making them "young before their time." "60 is the new 50" and other such age-based aphorisms are silly, I believe, as numbers should just stay out of the equation, but there is some truth to the idea that boomers look, act, and feel younger than their chronological years. Boomers are clearly redefining older age as they flood into their 60s and 70s, challenging prevailing notions about what "seniors" should be doing at that stage in their lives. Through physical and mental exercises, Eastern philosophies, and the power trio of sex, drugs, and roll, this first chapter shows, boomers are illustrating what the third stage of life can be about. Boomers may never truly get "old," at least in the way that we have traditionally defined that term, a legacy of their lifelong bond with youth. Given the revolutionary ways in which baby boomers are aging, this is a historic moment, we all should realize, and another contribution boomers have made to society.

OPPORTUNITY

Speak to boomers as if they were still young (at heart).

ANTIAGING

"What a drag it is getting old," Mick Jagger and Keith Richards wrote in their song "Mother's Little Helper" about a half century ago, perhaps not anticipating how much fun life could be as septuagenarians. (In July 2016, 72-year-old Jagger was reportedly delighted to learn that his 29-year-old ballerina girlfriend was pregnant with his child—his eighth.) Not just mothers but grandmothers (and grandfathers) are taking lots of little yellow helpers these days, however, with this widespread popping of pills being done not to calm down but in the pursuit to increase longevity, perhaps by decades. Gobbling dozens of pills is just one of many fountains of youth from which many boomers are drinking as they attempt to "antiage," that is, stop or slow the body's natural process of getting older.

Sadly, the media as well as marketers have both promoted the notion that getting older does not have to occur, contributing to the silly proposition that steps should be taken to circumvent aging. My local PBS station frequently airs antiaging shows such as *Aging Backwards*, for example, whose producers promise viewers that they can "reverse the aging process and look 19 years younger in 30 minutes a day." Olay, the maker of skincare products, urges consumers to look "ageless," an appeal that reflects our general antipathy toward getting older. Despite their popular appeal, "aging backwards" and "agelessness" are, of course, absurd concepts that have absolutely no foundation in how the human body or any other living organism works. Those who yearn to reverse the aging process are attempting to negate a fundamental part of life that every human in history has experienced. "Antiaging" is, quite simply, antihuman, making any and all efforts to achieve such a thing contrary to the basic mechanism of life as we know it.[1]

Despite all this, "antiaging" has emerged as a multibillion-dollar business, driven by boomers who have no intention to get physically old. Many boomers are fighting (versus embracing) the aging process, with the generation that defined (if not invented) youth culture largely resistant to the human body's insistence to do what it is programmed to do. "Antiaging" therapies are thus very popular, despite the fact that there is little or no evidence that any of them work, a sign of some boomers' desperate (and futile) attempt to cling to their physical youth. It's clear that consumers will do and pay virtually anything for something that promises to stop or reverse the aging process, with youth still perceived by many as the ultimate social currency.[2]

The ever-growing antiaging industry is only advancing our trepidation of getting older and reinforcing ageist inclinations. Precious little evidence has been produced to indicate that any therapy or technique slows or reverses the aging process yet, much to marketers' delight, consumers seem determined to find a fountain of youth. Modern day Ponce de Leons are following the tradition of many in the past in search of some magical treatment with purported rejuvenating powers. (In the 13th century, one of the great minds of the day, British mathematician and scientist Roger Bacon, maintained that sleeping next to a young virginal female in order to breathe in her wholesome air would restore youth.) Twenty-first-century versions of such therapies are nearly as silly and carry much greater potential health risks.[3]

One can only imagine how many Americans would be committed anti-agers if any treatment was proved to work over the long term and was determined to be completely safe. There is little or no clinical evidence that any of the popular methods being taken actually slow the aging process or add years to one's life. The demand for them, however, remains greater than ever. On a global basis, consumers spent almost $300 billion on all antiaging products and treatments in 2015, which included human growth hormone therapy, prescription or over-the-counter "smart drugs" (or nootropics), supplements such as DHEA, testosterone replacement, and vitamin and mineral infusions. Researchers had been able to slow aging in multicellular organisms and animals through a variety of other methods, but applying those learnings to humans remains just a dream, especially among those hoping to get rich from the realization of a fountain of youth.[4]

The recent entry of tech company executives, dot-com billionaires, and venture capitalists into the antiaging scene has taken the effort to an entirely new level. Wild success in this mortal world is not enough for these captains of industry who believe they can conquer nature through science and technology, not unlike how they conquered the universe of information. Billions will be spent by these techies on finding a solution to the problem of aging and, upon realizing it is a far more difficult undertaking than building a better browser or search engine, I believe they will return to doing what they do best—making money. Rather than promote the idea of antiaging, it is far wiser for marketers to take the high road by telling consumers that youth is more of a state of a mind than anything else. This is actually a more compelling (and truer) proposition than the oxymoronic, antihuman idea of "antiaging," and one that will help marketers avoid the coming backlash against claims promising the impossible.[5]

OPPORTUNITY

Tell boomers that youth is about what one does and how one feels versus how one looks.

BRAIN GAMES

Boomers may have more knowledge and wisdom than when they were younger because of life experience, but some of that brainy activity comes at a cost of speed and nimbleness. The most common cognitive changes are slowed processing speed—taking longer to work through a task or problem, making completion of daily tasks more challenging—and diminished working memory—the ability to hold, process, and mentally manipulate information. Reduced processing speed and working memory may affect attention and memory, as these higher level skills are necessary for concentration, efficiency of thought, as well as encoding and retrieval of information.[6]

While it is thus perfectly natural for mid-lifers to have "senior moments" once in a while ("And exactly why did I come into this room . . .?"), those and the fear of Alzheimer's are pushing many boomers to try to keep their brains young as they age. Seeing a very bright future ahead in cognitive health, more marketers are jumping into the "brain game" business by selling products that promise to slow or stop mental decline. The science behind the games seems dubious—people get better at playing them but there are no convincing signs that those improvements transfer to general mental skills or to everyday life—but the category continues to grow. According to one set of estimates, consumers spent $715 million on these games in 2013 and are set to spend $3.38 billion by 2020.[7] With some 50 million subscribers in almost 200 countries, lumosity.com is the most popular website to offer games for the brain, but there are others in the cognitive training business.[8] Happy Neuron claims to make possible "brain fitness for life,"[9] Cogmed promises that its system delivers "improved attention and capacity for learning,"[10] and Neuronix is in the process of creating something that offers "new hope for Alzheimer's disease."[11]

While scientists are unsure whether such brain games actually work—definitive proof that general thinking and memory are improved by performing a particular cognitive activity is lacking—all agree that the human brain continually develops new nerve-related linkages. That fact, and the common wisdom of "use it or lose it" in other areas of life, suggest that it does make sense that some kind of workout for the brain is a good idea to keep it from slowing down before it has to. There is some evidence that certain types of cognitive training—engaging in a brainteaser, learning a foreign language, or even advancing one's video game playing prowess—can be a positive factor in both the memory and concentration of older people. Most exciting, game training has triggered spikes in brain waves whose patterns resembled those in much younger people, suggesting that cognitive exercises can perhaps make boomers' thinking process sharper as they age.[12]

Given some anecdotal evidence that brain fitness courses may work, however, it's not surprising that a good number of boomers are signing up for them. Dakim BrainFitness and Saido Learning are just a couple of computer programs designed to sharpen memory and language abilities by giving the prefrontal cortex a workout, although anything that stimulates the brain might have the same effect. Seeing 60-somethings do increasingly complex written and verbal tasks on computers and iPads is becoming increasingly common, especially among those whose parents had some form of dementia. There is no evidence that brain games can help older adults avoid the onset of Alzheimer's if they are genetically inclined to do so, but that isn't stopping boomers from trying, just in case. Even doing the Sudoku puzzle in the newspaper may be the cognitive equivalent of a brisk walk for one's body, making such exercises a possible means toward a healthier brain by increasing what scientists call neuroplasticity. Neuroplasticity—the brain's ability to change with new learning and experiences—endures throughout the life span, making it possible for people of all ages to strengthen their cognitive abilities. Engaging in new learning by exposing oneself to new activities and intellectual challenges is the ideal way to improve brain health as we age.[13]

In fact, the latest research suggests that the best brain games are having a job that requires multifaceted thinking and interacting with others. These old standbys could assist in defending oneself against the onset of Alzheimer's, a couple of studies have shown, which is very exciting news given the potential epidemic America and the rest of the world is facing. A mentally stimulating lifestyle, whether professional or personal, appears to prevent cognitive decline, in other words, something older adults already knew intuitively. Keeping one's job as a lawyer, teacher, social worker, engineer, or doctor for as long as possible is thus a good recipe for mental health, more reason why ageism in the workplace has to be addressed as soon as possible. (Similar benefits can be gained by volunteering and mentoring.) "The development of Alzheimer's Disease or cognitive change with aging need not be a passive process," explained Ronald Petersen, the head of the Mayo Clinic Study of Aging, advising that "you can do something about it by staying intellectually active."[14]

> **OPPORTUNITY**
>
> Recognize that the real fountain of youth resides in working and playing with others.

EAST MEETS WEST

In 1968, the Beatles went to India to take part in a Transcendental Meditation (TM) session at the ashram of Maharishi Mahesh Yogi. Led by

George Harrison, the Beatles' interest in TM not only changed Western attitudes about Indian spirituality but ushered in a wholesale fascination with Eastern ways. Twenty-something baby boomers were most intrigued by the East, part and parcel of their countercultural notion of rejecting their parents' generation's way of life based in Western-style competition, conformity, and consumer capitalism. Buddhist philosophy meshed nicely with students' peace protests against the Vietnam War and achieving a state of bliss through TM and yoga (and psychedelics) became common among American youth culture.

A half century later, George Harrison's sitar is still ringing in boomers' ears. Eastern spiritualities have become mainstream, with boomers still finding Buddhism to be an ideal alternative or complement to traditional Judeo-Christian religion. "Meditation, dharma teachers, retreat centers and monasteries, as well as some core terms (dharma, karma, mindfulness, zazen, bodhisattva and metta, to name a few) have become well known and understood," observed writer and teacher Lewis Richmond, noting that most of the attendees at Buddhist centers are boomers.[15] With their early exposure to Eastern philosophies, boomers continue to embrace Buddhism and other alternative spiritualities as a means to feel, think, and act young.

Boomers are also showing their youthful alternative ways through Eastern health care practices. Right around the same time that boomers started chanting mantras to find inner peace, alternative medicine began to work its way across the West as well. Soon those with an open mind were taking natural medications instead of side-effect heavy pharmaceuticals, a movement that would eventually revolutionize the health care industry. Today, aging boomers with a growing number of health-related ailments are increasingly attracted to Eastern medicine for the very same reasons. Massage, acupuncture, herbal supplements, liquid vitamins, and essential oils are all part of this pursuit to stay healthy without resorting to drugs (and doctors). Boomers are cruising the aisles of CVS, Walgreen's, and Duane Reed for hawthorn and arjuna root for high blood pressure, red yeast rice and plant sterols for high cholesterol, curcumin and Glucosamine for joint pain, and ginger root for vertigo.[16]

Acupuncture—the Chinese practice of stimulating certain areas of the body, usually by putting narrow needles into the skin—is growing especially fast among boomers as a form of alternative medicine. Acupuncture can help those with certain conditions avoid surgery, and research from a study at the National Institutes of Health has shown that the technique is effective in reducing chronic pain. By literally pinpointing a half dozen energy points in the human body, acupuncture is said to reduce fatigue and help older people stay active for longer—just the fountain of youth boomers are seeking.[17]

Acupuncture is part of what some refer to as Traditional Chinese Medicine (TCM), which is expected to thrive in the years ahead as boomers get older. While Western science has yet to definitively prove that acupuncture has clinical efficacy, there is sufficient anecdotal evidence to suggest that it and other TCM modalities work. Unlike Western medicine, where a single doctor visit yields a prescription or referral, TCM works over time. The acceptance of Chinese medicine has been growing to the point where some insurance providers will cover treatments, however, good news for the millions of boomers who will inevitably have to deal with arthritis and other age-related chronic health conditions and diseases.[18]

As the *Wall Street Journal* reported over a decade ago, more boomers are also feeling younger through the low-impact fluid movements of qigong. The aim of qigong is to bring about "qi" (spoken as "chee"), the Chinese concept of curative energy that moves like a current throughout one's body. The workout of choice among Chinese peasants for thousands of years has definitely moved upmarket in recent years. The Sports Club/LA offers something called "SynerChi Sculpt," for example, which blends Eastern exercises like qigong with weight lifting, and The Spa at Turnberry Isle in Aventura, Florida, has made qigong part of its program. Prudential Financial and Mattel employees have attended sessions in qigong, and golf pros are keen on the ancient practice after hearing that Tiger Woods achieved his Zen-like state by studying it.[19]

Part of the popularity of qigong among boomers is that it is completely opposite from the kind of workout they likely did when they were younger. Participants follow a teacher engaged in deep breathing exercises combined with a set of flowing motions involving various parts of the body, especially the joint areas. The soaring interest in Eastern exercise practices like qigong is a function of boomers' desire to achieve fitness via a more integrated mind-body-spirit philosophy. Boomers are actually joining gyms in greater numbers than any other age group, so health clubs are sensibly responding by filling classes with kinder and gentler activities imported from Asia.[20]

OPPORTUNITY

Go East, marketer, to help boomers' maintain a sense of youthfulness.

SEX

With baby boomers having led the sexual revolution during the "free love" era of the 1960s and 1970s, sex is naturally seen by many of them as one source of their fountain of youth. "Sex was the hallmark of this generation's adolescent rebellion, and later on, a part of the women's movement we spearheaded," wrote sexologist Pepper Schwartz, adding that boomers were instrumental in making sex acceptable in popular culture and playing an important role in the gay civil rights movement. Schwartz and others are on a mission to help boomers navigate the sexual landscape as they age, not an easy thing for some. While surveys show that boomers of each gender subscribe to the idea that sex is vital and tend to remain active in that part of life (most older people believe sexuality is a key dimension of their relationships with their respective significant others), a variety of physical and emotional issues can make things difficult. It is not unusual for interest in sex to wane among women who are older than 50, for instance, and no product equivalent to those targeted at men's ED has yet to appear in the market.[21]

"So," Schwartz continues, "older adults, the same people who sparked and maintained a sexual revolution, are having to reinvent themselves again." Many boomers are recommitting themselves to sex, not about to give up on one of the best things in life because of physical or social challenges. About a third of the 65 million or so boomers are currently unmarried, making sex with new partners a part of the dating scene. Many boomers are caregivers to their elderly parents, but this sometimes serves as a way for them to meet new people. Hanging out at one's parents' nursing home has become the 21st-century version of the single's bar, as members of the sandwich generation hook up with each other in between caring for their mom or dad. Reconnecting with one's high school sweetheart via Facebook also is not unusual among single boomers, and some divorced couples are redefining their relationship as "friends with benefits." Married boomer couples face different issues when it comes to sex. Fifty- and 60-somethings are flocking to sex therapists, seeking ways to keep romance in their lives after being married for a quarter century.[22]

For some boomers, however, sex is way better now than it was while grooving to Marvin Gaye or Donna Summer. A few decades of experience, sometimes with many partners, has made sexagenarians live up to that term. Besides having learned some interesting positions over the years, sometimes with help from the *Kama Sutra*, older adults are less embarrassed to reveal their likes and fantasies to their lovers. Viagra, Cialis, and Levitra have of course revolutionized sex for older men and their partners. Plus, sex is now a lot more open than it was around the Bicentennial thanks to cable TV and the Internet, making certain activities that were then considered somewhat taboo perfectly normal.[23] Bisexuality too has come out of the closet over the past 40 years, opening up new sexual options for those who are so inclined. Sexual fluidity is virtually the new norm, in fact, as Gen Xers and millennials broke down the straight-or-gay barrier that had been in place for a very long time. Boomers, both men and women, are generally keen on pushing their respective sexual envelopes, interested in new and different experiences rather than the same old same old. The steamy bestseller *Fifty Shades of Gray* was a tipping point of sexuality, making many readers want to bring the explicitly erotic scenes in the novel to their own real-life bedrooms.[24]

Patty Brisben, founder of Pure Romance ("the world's leading and fastest-growing woman-to-woman direct seller of relationship-enhancement products"), has a deep understanding of the relationship between age and sexuality. While for some boomers a robust sex life may remind them of their youth, Brisben sensibly argues that people become "better" as they age, including their approach to and practice of sexuality. "Through experience, older adults develop a more complete sexual road map than their younger counterparts," she wrote in her blog for the *Huffington Post*'s Post 50, with a greater understanding of not just one's own body but others. Less inhibition, especially among women, and a relaxing of the standard of beauty defined by youth are just a couple of factors that make sex a lot more interesting for boomers than it is for 20-somethings. A new kind of confidence and comfort in one's own skin allows many older women to let it all hang out, so to speak, in the bedroom, Brisben and other sexologists report, a wonderful thing. And rather than having been-there-done-that intercourse, many couples who have been in long-term committed relationships will tell you that sex is better than ever, a function of the emotional and physical closeness they share with their partner.[25]

There are other good reasons to dispel the myth that boomers' best sexual days are behind them. For women, being post-menopausal means there's no chance of getting pregnant, one less thing to worry about if that's an issue. And if the kids are (finally) out of the house, there's more opportunity for spontaneous sex—the kind of sex couples used to have before the kids arrived. Romance too is often revived for empty nesters, further enhancing the sex lives of luckier baby boomers.[26]

> **OPPORTUNITY**
>
> Create products and services for boomers offering
> romance and intimacy.

DRUGS

Baby boomers were famous for smoking a doobie or two (or a kilo) back in the 1960s and 1970s but then they got jobs, spouses, and kids. For most, pot was replaced by the occasional glass of wine, although some boomers were known to still light up once in a while if the kids were at grandma's. Now, however, many boomers are going back to their heady days as marijuana becomes legal or decriminalized in many states and for a variety of other good reasons. For those boomers who abstained for a few decades, getting high makes them feel young again, reminding them of a time in their life when things did not have to be taken so seriously. The added plus is that rather than being a potential health risk, cannabis is now recognized as an excellent pain reliever for a host of ailments and as an anti-inflammatory that can also alleviate symptoms of some illnesses or medical conditions. Boomers shared joints during their first go round with pot, but this time they may very well be using it to sooth their aching joints.

Drugs are a serious problem for many, of course, but smoking the occasional reefer is for most a generally harmless recreational activity. It can be easily understood why boomers are enjoying high times once again. Alcohol is a depressant and can be over-consumed, while it is virtually impossible to overdose on marijuana. Many people are choosing strains of marijuana like Pink Panther or Glue Gorilla as their recreational drug of choice, believing weed to be less mind-numbing than alcohol. (See marijuanadictionary.com for a very full, extremely funny list of cannabis strains.) Reefer enhances rather than dulls thinking and creativity, or at least makes one feel that it does, another reason why it is becoming the drug of choice for people of all ages. Technological advances made since Grace Slick sang, "Feed your head" have made lighting up (or consuming it as an "edible") a lot more convenient. A vapor pen is not only discrete but eliminates the hassle of rolling a joint or loading a pipe (with one kind equipped for a little cartridge of liquid cannabis concentrate). With no fire, no smoke, and no odor to make one think you're at a Phish concert, you'd be surprised how many people are smoking pot rather than tobacco in their vape pens.[27]

All this has made the consumption of marijuana an opportunity for connoisseurship, not unlike that for wine or scotch. Strains that are classified as sativa deliver a more exultant, euphoric effect that is best for socializing or making humdrum chores like cleaning the house a lot more interesting. (Who knew that Scrubbing Bubbles could be so much fun?) Concentrates derived from indica strains are more sedating and good for couch potatoing. (*The Lord of the Rings Trilogy: Extended Edition* has recently been released on Blu-Ray, for those opting for this variety.) Many strains are categorized as hybrids, meaning they combine effects. (Perfect perhaps for cleaning the house while watching *The Lord of the Rings Trilogy: Extended Edition*.) A good budtender at a dispensary is a font of knowledge on the subject for those who live in a state where marijuana is legal, and there are a number of good apps and websites like Leafly.com that offer a tutorial in all thing weed.[28]

Stripped of its countercultural connotations, purchasing and consuming marijuana is now quite a different experience than it was decades ago, more reason for a significant number of boomers to rekindle their love affair with the plant. Often neatly packaged like any other product, marijuana is these days part of the establishment rather than a symbol of protest against it. Twenty states have so far made marijuana legal for medical use, and two states—Washington and Colorado—allow it to be consumed recreationally, with the debate about whether it should be available for those who want it virtually over. "It's not just long-haired rebels and stoners, but Mom and Dad," said Martin A. Lee, the author of *Smoke Signals*, a cultural history of the weed, in describing who's now lighting up. Using marijuana for medical reasons goes back thousands of years, and in this country it was a legitimate therapy from the mid-19th century to the 1930s when it was made illegal. Boomers made it a staple of their arsenal of substances to achieve altered states in the 1960s, and a couple of decades later those with AIDS discovered its helpful properties. That served as the basis for a movement to decriminalize use of marijuana for medical purposes, leading up to today's reefer madness.[29]

While recreational use of marijuana is a giant business unto itself, it is the plant's medical applications that have Big Pharma and Wall Street excited. The identification of varieties that contain cannabidiol or CBD, an element containing little THC (the psychoactive agent), has led to its use for both physical and mental conditions. Prescription-strength pot is readily available in those states where it has been declared legal for medical purposes, with users reporting it to be very effective for everything from nausea resulting from chemotherapy to chronic pain. Substances in marijuana are known to be palliative because of their chemistry, with research showing the weed can be particularly effective in alleviating the discomfort associated with arthritis. All in all, legal marijuana is projected to be a $10 billion industry by 2018, explaining why so many "ganjapreneurs" and investors (like Potbotics, a Palo Alto startup) are attracted to it.[30]

OPPORTUNITY

Dig up other alternative treatments that help boomers feel young and healthy.

ROCK 'N' ROLL

"Drummer seeking to form a classic rock band for fun and recreation in New Jersey. Guitars, bass, and vocalist(s) needed, keyboard welcome, too. Goal is to play once or twice a month, usually Sunday afternoons 1 to 5, and eventually perform for friends and family. Looking for fellow baby boomer 50s–60s age range. Stable folks only with day jobs, no drugs, no drama. The idea is to have fun. Rock on!"[31]

So reads an actual 2013 posting on patch.com. Classic rock is alive and well, as boomers play it, listen to it, or collect its ephemera in order to feel young. Classic rock is commercially popular music from the late 1960s to late 1980s, with that of the 1970s the definite sweet spot. Some boomers are forming classic rock garage bands with their buddies, perhaps returning to something they did when they were teenagers dreaming of becoming the next Led Zeppelin or The Doors. As the aforementioned New Jerseyite makes clear, however, getting a group together this time is purely for kicks, with no professional aspirations whatsoever. The process is sometimes not unlike that of the Blues Brothers, who search for old mates to reunite an old band (while not being on a mission from God), or instead cobble together a new band through networking. Musicians start practicing in a garage or basement (often much to their spouses and/or kids' dismay) and, after a few months perhaps, feel ready to play at a barbecue or party. There are some recognizable songs, but more often than not sets evolve (or more accurately devolve) into a jam session disturbingly similar to that depicted in the new incarnation of Spinal Tap when they "do a free-form jazz exploration in front of a festival crowd." Still, a good time is always had by all, especially the boys (and sometimes girls) in the band who feel like they're 16 again.[32]

Way back in 1983, Houston radio station KRBE radio was the first in the United States to employ the phrase "Classic Rock" in describing the kind of music it was broadcasting. The station aired rock 'n' roll produced only between the 1960s and early 1970s when research showed that many boomers disliked the synthesizer-heavy New Wave music that was taking over the airwaves. The rest, as they say, is history. Classic rock is more popular than ever and is showing no signs of becoming obsolete. Hundreds of contemporary bands come and go, but groups whose creativity peaked around Watergate still tour to packed crowds. Sales of recorded music industry is a fraction of what they once were thanks to the Internet, but a good percentage of the CDs and vinyl that does sell is classic rock songs and albums. Classic rock radio, both terrestrial and satellite, is huge, with listeners apparently never tiring of hearing songs by the likes of Aerosmith, AC/DC, Boston, Kansas, Heart, ZZ Top, Kiss, and Queen. All generations listen to classic rock, but boomers account for most of the audience, as they loved the music when it was brand new. Research shows that people most clearly remember that period of time when they were in their twenties and assign the strongest emotional connections to that age as well. For most boomers, that was the 1970s, explaining why not just music of the decade but much of its popular culture is still around today.[33]

Collectors also find classic rock to be a fountain of youth. The digital age has fueled the interest for all things analog, especially for memorabilia of the two-decade era. Scraps of old scribbled lyrics are selling for thousands of dollars and sometimes more. (Don McLean's "American Pie" manuscript from 1971, which had been found in the trash, was recently auctioned off for $1.2 million.) With lots of disposable money, boomers are investing in the paper and vinyl trail of classic rock, especially that produced for the most popular bands like the Grateful Dead and the Beach Boys. Unlike a music file, posters, T-shirts, and album covers are tangible, and serve as vivid reminders of a defining moment in time for many boomers.[34]

Some very rich boomers, notably Paul Allen, Microsoft cofounder and owner of the Seattle Seahawks, and Jim Irsay, who owns the Indianapolis Colts, are avid collectors of rock 'n' roll memorabilia. Irsay recently purchased Ringo Starr's circa-1963 Ludwig drum kit at an auction for $2.25 million (he's also the proud possessor of the Stratocaster Dylan played at the Newport Festival and the one-of-a-kind Tiger guitar previously owned by Jerry Garcia). Allen, meanwhile, founded the Experience Music Project Museum in Seattle, the biggest holder of Jimi Hendrix and Kurt Cobain artifacts in the world. At a recent Sotheby's auction, an anonymous collector snagged the groovy Porsche 356 Cabriolet once driven by Janis Joplin for $1.76 million, while Kurt Cobain's grungy mohair cardigan sold for $137,500 and the guillotine used in Alice Cooper's shows went for a downright cheap $32,500. "In some strange convergence of economics, sentiment and availability, wealthy baby boomers looking for interesting places to park their money occupy a historical moment in which the elders of rock's greatest generation have realized they can't take it with 'em," *Newsweek* reported in 2016, adding that "rock 'n' roll's history, it seems, is being bought up by the 1 percent."[35] One doesn't have to be rich to play or listen to classic rock or to collect less rare artifacts from the era, however, ensuring that the music will remain the soundtrack of boomers' lives.

OPPORTUNITY

Make boomers feel young by revisiting popular culture
from their youth.

TWO

Old Dog, New Tricks

Learning is an ongoing experience; it's not particular to a specific life stage, but significant and meaningful for all.

Mai Kobori of Parsons School of Design

In the hilarious 1986 movie *Back to School*, Thornton Melon, played by the indefatigable Rodney Dangerfield, enrolls in his son's college as a rather extraordinary act of parental guidance. His son Jason is thinking about dropping out, so Melon, a street-smart, uneducated, hard-partying, rags-to-riches millionaire, donates big bucks to the university in order to be able to attend classes. Hijinks naturally ensue, with Melon hiring a team of intellectuals (including Kurt Vonnegut in a cameo) to do his schoolwork. The dean of the university (named Dean Martin, of course) threatens to expel Melon when he learns of his academic shenanigans and makes him take a difficult oral exam to stay in school. Melon crams for the test (the dean asks one question in 27 parts) and, with some help from his son and others, he passes, showing that anyone can succeed at anything if they work hard enough.[1]

Melon may not be your average student ("At the high school I went to, they asked a kid to prove the law of gravity, and he threw the teacher out the window!" he says), but many people of a certain age are indeed going back to school and pursuing knowledge of all kinds. "Baby boomers bring new meaning to the term lifelong learner," declared Ali Durkin of Northwestern University in reporting the rise of older adults in higher education and as they gain greater proficiency in a plethora of specialized areas.[2] Old dogs are learning new tricks, one might say, as boomers satisfy their thirst to know more about some aspect of the world for professional or personal reasons.

Boomers' expansion of their gray matter is grounded in research dispelling the myth that cognition declines with age. Contrary to popular belief, older people are perfectly capable of learning new things, with study after study showing that the human brain continues to generate new cells as it ages. Research also suggests that older brains do best when exposed to intellectual stimuli, making the idea of use-it-or-lose-it especially true for aging cerebral cortexes. Fortunately, as the most highly educated generation in history (until millennials came along), boomers are very interested in continuing to learn and try new things and will remain curious about the world throughout their third act.

Formal education is just one way boomers are proactively pursuing new forms of knowledge. Travel can be an education in itself, of course, with little in life more exciting than gaining some familiarity with a different culture. As well, a good percentage of boomers' commitment to learning has to do with completing something they had begun when they were much younger, time now being on their side. Finally, many of boomers' learning opportunities are holistic in nature, meaning they combine aspects of the mental, physical, and spiritual selves. Whatever the particular avenue of learning, boomers are throwing themselves in head (or body) first, making their third act perhaps the most rewarding and fulfilling time in their lives.

OPPORTUNITY

Leverage older dogs' wish to learn new tricks in their third act.

CONTINUING EDUCATION

Continuing education has been around for decades, of course, but baby boomers are turning it into something much bigger and better. While seniors of past generations took classes as a fun pastime, 55+ers of today are likely doing it for more practical reasons. The leading motive for boomers to pursue additional education is to acquire new, career-related skills, a recent AARP survey reported, with other professional reasons being to make more money, increase opportunities of promotion, or complete a degree. As the next chapter will show, many boomers are "rebooting" in some way, with additional education often the means to open a new chapter in their lives. Embarking on a new career or deciding to give back some way typically takes skills one doesn't yet possess, making continuing education a growing area for schools of all kinds. Three trends—the age wave, increased longevity, and boomers' love of learning—are creating a kind of perfect storm within education, a good thing by any measure.[3]

The stories involving boomers going back to school reflect the diversity of the group. Now having both time and money, doctors and lawyers in their sixties are enrolling in divinity schools as they turn their attention to more spiritual matters. Others who have been downsized after decades of working at a particular company are earning college degrees to begin an "encore" career, such as teaching. Executive MBA programs are literally booming as boomers tune up their business skills, sometimes to better compete with younger employees. Those without a bachelor's degree are finally getting around to it, in the process realizing what often was a lifelong dream. Happily, many colleges and universities are offering low—or no-cost continuing education programs to older adults. The GO-60 program offered by Penn State Continuing Education at University Park, for example, provides courses at no cost to Pennsylvania residents who are 60 years old or more and are not fully employed. GO-60 students experience courses alongside undergraduate students and can take them for credit or audit, a much easier path than Thornton Melon had to travel in his thankfully fictional version of going back to school.[4]

The New School in New York clearly understands the kinds of new tricks more creative old dogs are interested in learning based on its program in continuing education. "What's your educational dream?" it asks potential, multigenerational students, "to learn how to speak French, write your first novel, or maybe even design your own fashion line?" Much like the students, the courses at The New School are heterogeneous and deliver on the program's tagline, "Unparalleled Creativity. Relentlessly Relevant." At Parsons School of Design, for example, one can take classes in design and art, while the Mannes School of Music specializes in that subject. Students can take credit or noncredit classes at the Schools of Public Engagement to earn a certificate or enroll in online courses in an almost infinite array of subjects. For those determined to embark on some creative professional path, The New School offers flexible learning opportunities that traditional degree programs do not, something well suited for boomers wishing that their third act is an artistic one.[5]

While The New School is probably the sexiest of continuing education options for boomers, it is community colleges that do the heavy lifting. Many community colleges across the country are making a proactive effort to reach the boomer market, knowing that it represents a huge growth opportunity for them. Two-year colleges are well positioned to meet the educational needs of older students, as they lean more toward practical career training (or retraining) than the kind of ivory tower thinking typically found in abundance at four-year colleges. "To meet future demands, we need to prolong the labor force participation of aging baby boomers," Mary Sue Vickers of the American Association of Community Colleges (AACC) noted, adding that "we need to increase educational opportunities for the current work force."[6]

Vickers is the director of the AACC's Plus 50 Initiative, a program currently being adopted by colleges across the country to help over-50 students make a smooth transition to and succeed in a college setting. The Plus 50 Initiative, which was begun in 2008, is specifically designed to help community colleges provide for older learners by offering the tools and knowledge those colleges need to attract and engage a wider demographic of students. The initiative benchmarks and showcases the best programs at community colleges targeted to students 50 years old or older so that other schools could develop similar ones. The initiative also provides financial support to community colleges to develop additional programs catering to older learners, especially those that can help pave the way for new opportunities in the workplace. Over the past decade, Plus 50 has awarded grants to over a hundred community colleges having a total enrollment of more than 37,000 older students, each one interested in using their education to launch a new career. The program has made a major contribution to the professional lives of older learners, with more than 12,000 individuals earning a certificate or degree over the past six years.[7] Expect community colleges to steal some of large universities' thunder in the years ahead as they cater to boomers' educational needs.

OPPORTUNITY

Go to school on continuing education by helping
boomers get smarter.

HARVARD ADVANCED LEADERSHIP INITIATIVE

Speaking of smartness, Harvard University is blazing the trail of a limited number of baby boomers' intellectual future through its Advanced Leadership Initiative (ALI). The ALI, created by Rosabeth Moss Kanter,

Rakesh Khurana, and Nitin Nohria (all professors at the university), is "a bold, academic innovation that has the potential to become another facet of higher education, change the concept of 'retirement' and help change the world for the better," Harvard explains, something very much in sync with many boomers' own plans for their third act. The ALI is "a new third stage in higher education designed to prepare experienced leaders to take on new challenges in the social sector where they potentially can make an even greater societal impact than they did in their careers," it adds. By educating and deploying into public service those who've already achieved great things, the thinking goes, solutions to huge global challenges like poverty, health care, conservation efforts, and education can potentially be found. Research universities like Harvard are "uniquely positioned to close knowledge gaps by finding new ways to develop and implement comprehensive solutions through integrative research and educational innovation," the ALI acknowledges, its mission a perfect example of how such an institution can achieve such mighty goals.[8]

Through the ALI, a portion of boomers' lofty countercultural dream of creating a more just world is finally becoming realized. By "tapping the experience of a socially conscious generation of leaders and helping them redirect and broaden their skills to fill critical leadership gaps," the ALI declares, there is a greater chance of solving major social issues in which a simple, one-off approach has not been effective. Beginning in 2009, a hand-picked team of fellows of various backgrounds with impressive credentials came to Harvard to segue from their day job to hopefully become a "change agent for society." Over the course of their one-year gig at Harvard, ALI Fellows immerse themselves in the outstanding intellectual pickings of the university in order to prepare for their personal ALI ambitions. The skills of these folks (who have nothing to prove at this point in their careers) are then enhanced and leveraged, with graduates better prepared to address social problems in this new and exciting part of their professional lives.[9]

The stories of representative ALI graduates prove that the fellowship is more than a nice idea steeped in classic boomer idealism. At age 57, for example, Doug Rauch had spent 30 years at the grocery chain Trader Joe's, the last 14 as president. After attending ALI, he founded Daily Table, a nonprofit store in Dorchester, Massachusetts, where fresh, healthy foods are sold at affordable prices to those who otherwise would not be able to buy them. "We have got massive amounts of wasted food, and, at the same time, we have got 49 million Americans that can't afford to eat properly," Rauch told *PBS News* in 2016, tackling that big problem by sourcing excess inventory, grabbing products with a shorter code date, or making special buys. More than 200 former executives like Rauch have attended ALI, and in 2016 there were 47 fellows. One of them was Suneel Kamlani, who had served as the COO at the investment bank UBS and aims to bring in capital from the private sector to help rebuild the country's crumbling infrastructure. Biotech entrepreneur Ken Kelley, meanwhile, is in the process of creating a partnership between the public and private sectors that will seed a worldwide investment fund in order to make available drugs and vaccines for overlooked tropical diseases like Ebola before they turn into epidemics. Lynne Wines, an ex-banker, intends to assist adults with cognitive issues such as dyslexia to become employed, a wonderful idea.[10]

The ALI's mission speaks for itself:

- "To establish a new stage of higher education, as a collaboration across disciplines and professions, that will deploy a new leadership force of experienced leaders transitioning from their income-earning years to their next years of service;
- To pioneer in life-long learning for late-stage learners who will use the knowledge to change society and its institutions, individually and collectively making a difference on global, national, and community problems;
- To ensure that this mission of serving the world contributes to a great University for the future; and
- To help shape and contribute to a growing body of knowledge about how to change society at the system or institutional level, through innovations that improve education, health, environmental stewardship, urban revitalization, human rights and access to justice, and other complex multi-stakeholder issues benefiting from leadership that can work across professions and disciplines."[11]

OPPORTUNITY

Join forces with ALI Fellows to help make the world a better place.

LANGUAGE IMMERSION

Versus other peoples, Americans are notoriously unilinguistic, but that is gradually changing as our nation becomes more multicultural. Not just millennials but baby boomers are part of this shift toward a more polyglot country. Boomers who might have taken Spanish or French in high school but never became fluent are recommitting themselves to learning a language other than English, a function of having some time on their hands and a desire to keep their brains expanding in some way. For the average adult, learning a new language is not all easy. Young children have 50 percent more synapses (neurological connections) than the number in an adult brain, part of the reason kids less than six years old soak up language like a sponge. Adult brains are wired for different things than learning languages, and fluency in one makes picking up another actually harder.[12]

Perhaps because learning a new language is such a challenge for older people, immersion is often the only way to go for those truly wishing to become multilingual. More determined boomers are spending considerable time with self-instruction systems like Fluenz or Rosetta Stone and then going to a language meet-up group to practice what they learned. Intensive classes and keeping one's television tuned to a channel in a foreign language are other typical parts of the immersion process. Finally, one feels ready to travel to a country where the language is spoken to test one's skills. Sadly, for many, one quickly realizes that one sounds more like Borat trying to speak English rather than a native.[13]

There is a cognitive bonus for those who don't master a new language despite their best efforts, however. Working one's brain so hard often improves both verbal and visual memory, researchers are finding, especially for older adults. Language study mimics various other cognitive tasks, making the difficult process kind of a CrossFit workout for the brain. As the last chapter showed, brain fitness programs like Nintendo's Brain Age and Lumosity and are getting a lot of attention among boomers worried about possible mental decline, but trying to learn a new language, even if unsuccessful, can apparently improve one's cerebral chops.[14]

Many boomers are combining their desire to learn a new language with their other passion of travel. After some initial prep work at home, older dogs are heading to places to not only gain linguistic proficiency in a language they like but to immerse themselves in a different culture. Diving headfirst into an alternative universe increases the odds that one will achieve fluency or something in the vicinity. "A culturally immersive program, where it is not possible to speak English, is the only way to learn a new language, in my opinion," posits Irene Lane, the founder of Greenloons, an eco-adventure company. Greenloons offers immersive global journeys for those wanting an "authentic" vacation experience that provides a real sense of place. France and Italy are understandably popular destinations, but a surprising number of well-traveled boomers are opting for places like Kenya, where they can learn Masai. Visitors observe how the locals live and get the chance to interact with all kinds of people for an experience that goes well beyond that by staying in a resort for tourists. For travelers short on time, Greenloons offers short-term trips to learn a particular language, such as taking classes in colloquial Hebrew at a café in Tel Aviv or being tutored in business-speak Spanish at the Academia Hispano Americana, a language academy in San Miguel. One takes home from such an amazing journey not just a trinket but the far more valuable ability to communicate in a different way and see the world from a different perspective—precisely the kind of learning experience many boomers are after at this point in their lives.[15]

Those wishing to speak a foreign tongue might want to know that there are a number of factors involved in how easy or difficult the process will likely be. How close the new language is to English plays an important role, as does the relative complexity of that language. Languages closely related to English are Norwegian, Afrikaans, Swedish, Dutch, Romanian, Italian, French, Portuguese, and Spanish, but one will still have to spend about six months and 600 class hours to achieve proficiency. Languages with significant differences from English include Finnish, Hebrew, Greek, Serbian, Thai, Polish, Turkish, Vietnamese, Russian, and Hindi, meaning it will require learners about 11 months and 1,100 class hours to become competent. Only the truly dedicated dare to try to learn those languages that are difficult for native English speakers to pick up, as it will likely take about 20 months and 2,200 class hours. Those include Arabic (which has very few words that resemble those of European languages and uses fewer vowels), Chinese (which is a tonal language with many characters and has a complicated writing structure), Japanese (which also requires memorizing thousands of characters and has three different writing systems and two syllable systems), and Korean (which has different sentence structure, syntax, and verb conjugations).[16] Still, lots of boomers are taking classes in Mandarin to be better prepared for a more Chinese-centric future (just like their grandchildren!).

OPPORTUNITY

Figure out ways to help boomers improve their brains as they age.

MUSIC LESSONS

Picture your typical music student: a boy or girl maybe eight years old, nervously tapping out "Old McDonald" on a piano with his or her tiny fingers. That picture hasn't changed, but a much different kind of student is now also likely to be taking music lessons. Many baby boomers who always wanted to be able to play an instrument are finally learning how, in the process helping their brain in a similar way that studying a new language does. Playing a musical instrument is one of the few activities that give one's brain a total workout, thus serving as a great way to keep one's mind sharp as it ages. Moving a set of drumsticks or violin bow at the right time and in the right place is more complicated than one might think, requiring an orchestrated set of firing neurons. Practicing an instrument just a couple of hours a week over the course of four to five months benefits both auditory processing and motor skills significantly, a mind-body connection that is ideal for aging bodies.[17]

With memory loss understandably a major concern for aging boomers, it's not surprising that many are seeking ways to preserve and perhaps even improve their cognitive skills. Research shows that playing music increases not only one's memory but focus and intelligence by actually reshaping and adding power to the brain. People who play music have organizationally and functionally different brains from those who do not, with some science suggesting that playing music can increase one's IQ by seven points. Adult brains are still quite malleable, meaning it's never too late to start learning to play music. And if hearing a song can make an individual happy or sad, playing an instrument has the power to completely alter one's emotional state. Because creating harmony and melody demands intense concentration, one's heart rate tends to slow down while playing music (heavy metal an exception, perhaps). Studies have shown that playing music actually reduces stress on a molecular level, making it kind of a natural Prozac.[18]

Many such boomers were effectively forced to play an instrument as a child, but this time it's a whole different story. Students in their fifties or sixties now get to pick the instrument of their choice rather than have to try to play that clarinet or bassoon they were handed in second grade. Music teachers also tend to be a lot kinder and gentler to older students than the ones who seemed to be always barking out things like "Nyet!" in a Russian accent, while sitting next to terrified children. Going at the pace one prefers is another advantage over the once or twice a week lessons scheduled while one's friends played happily outside. Finally, choosing which tunes to play is a lot more enjoyable than having to play, say, Rachmaninoff's Symphony #1 or Shostakovich's sixth concerto after doing scales for half an hour.[19]

Music schools are seeing an influx of boomer students wanting to learn how to play an instrument as a creative outlet, for socialization purposes, to improve their brain health, or just for fun. At the Longy School of Music in Cambridge, Massachusetts, for example, 200 adult students are taking group classes or individual lessons. At about $100 an hour, private instruction does not come cheap; group classes are more reasonable at $40 each. Like the Boston area, New York is rich with musical education opportunities for older adults. The Greenwich House Music School, for example, has 100 adult students, each paying around $70 an hour and almost all of them studying piano. "They have the time and money to be able to come back and do this kind of thing," the director of the school explained, hitting the nail on the head. In addition to music schools, boomers are going to their local music store to take lessons, especially in guitar. Contacting university music departments is a good way to find a teacher catering to older adults, and there are innumerable websites offering online instruction or DVDs. Skypeing or FaceTiming with a teacher is an increasingly popular way to learn music (or anything else).[20]

No website offering online instruction in music is more innovative than ArtistWorks, which is "dedicated to providing anyone, anywhere in the world with affordable, interactive access to some of the greatest music teachers in the world." The mission of the company is to "Teach the World Music" through its (patented) Video Exchange Learning Platform, which puts expert teachers together with eager players in an online learning setting that the company claims is unique to the industry. Every one of the handpicked teachers has deep experience in all relevant aspects of the music business, which they pass on to players of all skill levels. ArtistWorks' platform is supported by a giant library of fundamental lessons that leads members from the basics to sophisticated techniques in drums, vocal, ukulele, mandolin, guitar, piano, saxophone, cello, dobro, bass, banjo, fiddle, art, flute, clarinet, French horn, trumpet, violin, percussion, scratch, and harmonica. If players have questions or having trouble working through a particular passage, ArtistWorks' technology permits them to post practice videos and then receive personal video replies from their teacher. Face-to-face music lessons will no doubt always be around, but such technology points to the future of learning in all kinds of fields.[21]

OPPORTUNITY

Develop proprietary ways to interface with boomers.

MARTIAL ARTS

Snatch the pebble from my hand, little grasshopper. So went the title sequence to the 1970s television series *Kung Fu*, in which Kwai Chang Caine, a young martial arts student, proves he has the skills and wisdom to leave school and make his way into the outside world. Perhaps inspired by the Shaolin monk who flees China to roam America's Wild West to defend the helpless by karate chopping bad guys (while trying to track down his half-brother and elude bounty hunters), a good number of baby boomers are heading to dojos to learn the martial arts.[22] (For those wondering, "kung fu" roughly translates not into "ridiculous TV show" but rather "skill achieved through hard work.")[23] Sixty-somethings may not have the same way of the tiger or sign of the dragon as Caine, but they are pursuing the ancient form of combat as a means of self-defense, excellent workout, exercise in mental focus, or path of spirituality.

At places like Dynamic Martial Arts in South Dakota, for example, Karate for Boomers is just the thing for those perhaps wishing they had earned a black belt back in the day but now want a different kind of martial arts experience. Unlike jujitsu, which is like a WWE (World Wrestling Entertainment) Smackdown match, karate has minimal takedowns and is more structured, making it ideal for those not wanting to end up in the ER. At Dynamic and hundreds of other martial arts studios across the country, boomers are likely to learn Shorin Ryu, the 1,000-year-old Okinawan system of karate based on patterns (called "katas") of blocks, kicks, and strikes with the hands and feet. Shorin Ryu is essentially a gymnastics floor exercise, providing basic self-defense techniques, a chance to get into shape, and discipline.[24] With its Baby Boomer Martial Arts Class, Dragon Kim's Karate USA in Staten Island, New York, offers a traditional martial arts practice but with less bodily stress and lower impact on joints, an excellent example of longevity marketing.[25]

Things are taken a bit more seriously at the Green Hill Martial Arts Academy in Killingworth, Connecticut. The mission of the academy is to teach people to protect themselves against any conceivable method of aggression anywhere, anytime via tools for self-defense for everyone in everyday situations. The school specializes in Combat Hapkido or *Chon-Tu Kwan*, a relatively new, vigorous form that provides the best of traditional martial arts but skips all the formality of the latter. Combat Hapkido concentrates on the joints (manipulation and locking), below-the-waist kicks, targeted hits, weapon takeaways, and down-and-dirty survival tricks—all intended to control an opponent with what is pleasantly described as "pain compliance." With no spinning jump kicks, breaking of boards, lightning-quick punches, or tournaments, this martial art has little to do with the one seen in *The Karate Kid*. Combat Hapkido is well suited for older adults because rather than relying on physical strength or great athletic abilities, it uses the energy of an attacker (hence "Hapkido," the Korean word for "The Way of Joined Energy"). Because every attack is unique and the defender's tactics are never predetermined, the overall goal of Combat Hapkido is to develop a flexible mind and the spontaneity and creativity to make quick and appropriate responses to hostile actions (which happened to be the philosophy of the late martial arts icon Bruce Lee).[26]

Besides learning how to handle oneself in a street fight, practicing one of the dozens of martial arts makes considerable sense for those boomers who have run their last marathon but still want to stay fit. Movements improve strength, stamina, flexibility, and coordination, all things that are good for aging bodies. Workouts begin with warm-up exercises and then usually proceed to sparring, with a memorization component or "form work" an essential part of the process. In martial arts, a form is a series of choreographed movements the student must learn and execute in order to proceed through the levels of the discipline, with the intricacy of the forms increasing as the student progresses. Rather than being just a set of tech- niques learned and practiced in a studio a few times a week, however, mar- tial arts is a lifestyle or even philosophical pursuit, making it much more than the typical workout at the gym. As a solo discipline within a group setting, the arts offer comradeship without competition, this too setting it off from the standard beat-the-other-guy-before-he-beats-you approach of Western sports.[27]

In addition to karate, there are a few other martial arts that are popular with boomers because of their emphasis on groundwork and learning how to use an attacker's superior speed and strength to one's advantage. Taekwondo is a Korean discipline that blends a focus on self-discipline with various combat and self-defense movements, while judo is a more recent art of Japanese origin that emphasizes subduing an attacker rather than causing them serious injury. Aikido is another "soft" art with a self-defense orientation, that is, using a more powerful enemy's advan- tages against them through joint locks and trapping. Not every form of martial arts, studio, or program is right for everyone, making it important for students of all age to find the school that is most in line with their goals.[28]

OPPORTUNITY

Combine East and West in your own business as a best-of-both-worlds strategy.

PICKLEBALL

No, it's not a trendy appetizer involving an orb-shaped, marinated cucumber. Rather, Pickleball is, as many 55+ers already know, a game or sport that is especially suited for them. Pickleball is a cross among badminton, tennis, and table tennis played on an inside or outside 20-foot by 44-foot court (within a regulation size tennis court) and is all the rage at parks, rec centers, and communities composed of "active adults." Two players (or, more often, four players in teams of two) bat around Whiffle balls with paddles that look like supersized table tennis racquets, with the rules of the game and the height of the net close to those of tennis. Sounds strange, maybe, especially for tennis enthusiasts, but anyone who has played Pickleball (including me) will tell you it's a helluva lot of fun and a great workout. The number of people playing Pickleball is rising fast and will continually do so as millions more folks look for a sport that requires considerable moving around, sharp reflexes, and good balance and agility but with a low risk of injury. Not just tennis but racquetball, skiing, and even golf are hard on the body, meaning lower impact sports will thrive in the years and decades ahead. Likewise, gym equipment like treadmills can strain knees (and are boring), another reason for the meteoric ascent of pickleball.[29]

The basic rules and strategy of pickleball closely resemble those of other racquet sports. Unlike tennis, however, the serve has to be delivered underhand, and one must strike the ball with the paddle below the waist or bellybutton. Like tennis, the serve is sent crosscourt (diagonally) and has to bounce inside the kitty corner service box (but unlike tennis, just a single serve is permitted). Scoring points is limited to the team that is serving, with games usually played to 11 points (and won by 2). Dinks (a soft shot hit on a bounce and intended to arc over the net) and drop shots (a soft shot hit off a bounce from deep in the court and intended to land close to the net, i.e., the opponent's "kitchen") are key strategies of the game. Like tennis, there are groundstrokes, volleys, lobs, and overhead smashes, making it a relatively easy transition for players of that game.[30]

For those who equate Pickleball with shuffleboard or other sports associated with geezers, think again. With the ball not bouncing nearly as high as the one in tennis and the ability to put some monster spin on it, Pickleball requires one to be quick on one's feet. Many boomers are adopting it as their new physical activity of choice, knowing that they'll be able to play it for most of the rest of their lives. Pickleball is competitive but, perhaps because the court is smaller (and the name so peculiar), far more social than tennis. Foursomes typically get together two or three times a week for a couple of hours, with drinks following the game almost de rigueur. For whatever reasons, nice, friendly people tend to be drawn to the game, precisely the kind of social network many boomers are seeking as they head into their third act. Pickleballers are apt to recruit those who have yet to play it as if on a missionary quest, a reflection of the passion they feel for the game. In fact, there are over 1,400+ official ambassadors for the sport who are part of, yes, the United States of America Pickleball Association.[31]

Although many still have not heard of it, Pickleball has been around for some time. Three fathers whose children were keen on a new summertime activity conceived the game in 1965 on Bainbridge Island (a quick trip by ferry from Seattle, Washington). The game has grown considerably since then. There are now more than 2.5 million pickleball participants in the United States playing on over 15,000 indoor and outdoor courts in nearly 4,500 locations (with at least one location in all 50 states), according to the 2016 Participant Report put out by the Sports & Fitness Industry Association (SFIA). Over the last few years, there has been an explosion of new court construction throughout the country, especially in the southern states. Accounts of how the name originated differ, although many credit one of the game's inventors who owned a dog named Pickles for coming up with it. (Pickles apparently liked to run around on the court as much as the kids.)[32]

Across the country, empty tennis courts are being filled to the gills with avid pickleballers and gym floors being repainted with the game's court lines. Some tennis courts are being converted for pickleball, the nice thing being that the latter requires just a fourth of the former's court size.[33] And versus waiting around for someone to show up with whom to play tennis, pickleball courts are often surrounded by people with paddles in hand. The ability to play at no or low cost is another plus for the game.[34] "Pickleball is taking Orange County—and the nation—by storm," the *Orange County Register* declared in 2016, as players from Dana Point to Seal Beach join the game.[35] With such media reports, some pickleball proponents claim it to be as the fastest growing sport in the world, and that it will down the road become our new national pastime. While that might be hyperbole, many pickleballers claim to be either "obsessed" or "addicted" with the game, something not usually heard regarding any recreational activity, particularly those played by older people.[36]

OPPORTUNITY

Don't underestimate boomers' desire to learn new things.

THREE

Reboot

Everything changes, nothing remains without change.

Buddha

In 2006, when I was 50 years old, I thought I was done, metaphorically speaking. My consulting business had fizzled out, and my girlfriend of 10 years had left me as I wasn't ready to get married and start a family. Also, the winters and chaos of New York City, where I was living at the time, were beginning to get to me, more reason to consider making a major life change. Fortunately, I had a little nest egg and know how to live cheaply, so coasting, for the lack of a better word, for the rest of my life seemed like an attractive option. After weighing the pros and cons of warmer places that I liked—Miami, New Orleans, Austin, and Los Angeles—I bought a little art deco condo in South Beach and was soon happily spending my days writing books in flip-flops and my nights partaking in the never-ending party scene. I'd spend summers in Manhattan or the Hamptons, even if it involved simply crashing on someone's sofa for a few months.

So much for well-laid plans. Just a year or so after living the life I truly believed I would never want to change (why would one?), I met a woman who made me start to rethink my future. A few years into that relationship (I move rather slowly in that department, obviously), I gave up the partying (but not the writing) and agreed to try to have a baby with her. One year later I became a father and two years after that got married, making my life completely different than what I had envisioned it was going to be. Now, at 60, I spend most of my time with my daughter, an immensely joyous experience, but one that carries far more responsibility and commitment than I ever thought possible. I'm also consulting again and have rekindled my love affair with New York City, more reason to recognize that the expression "never say never" is a very wise one indeed.

What the hell happened to me? Well, to put it succinctly, I rebooted, turning off my old life and starting a new one, something that is in fact not that all unusual among baby boomers like myself. Contrary to popular belief, boomers are just as amenable to making major life changes when situations call for them, whether they involve work, relationships, where to live, romance, or spirituality. Whether carefully planned out or serendipitous, rebooting is about looking forward rather than backward, challenging the idea that boomers spend most of their time remembering better days when they were young, as older people of generations past might have. Popular culture about baby boomers is overly nostalgic, making it seem like they represent a chapter in American history rather than a group of people who are still leading active, interesting lives. While it's true that many boomers are not reluctant to tell their kids (or anyone else) about how they got arrested at a sit-in to protest the Vietnam War, stayed up super late to see the first men walk on the moon (I did), or saw Led Zeppelin on their first North American concert tour in late 1968 and early 1969 (opening for Vanilla Fudge, Iron Butterfly, or Country Joe & Fish, incredibly), the group is actually more interested in what lies ahead in the future than in what happened in the past.

OPPORTUNITY

Think of boomers as a work in process open to new experiences.

UNRETIREMENT

For many Americans of the postwar generation, the idea of retirement was nothing less than a dream come true. One day, usually at age 65, people would stop working and begin a life of leisure, knowing that Social Security and whatever savings they had managed to accumulate over the years would be enough to live on. With life expectancy in the United States 67 for men and 74 for women in 1965, after all, one didn't need too much money to get through, on average, the next couple of years or decade. In addition, Medicare, the national social insurance, began that year, with the federal government now picking up the medical and hospital tab for Americans 65 or older. Supported by the government entitlements of Social Security and Medicare, most older Americans could at least squeak by, enjoying their final years bouncing grandchildren on their knee, going out for early dinner at a local eatery, and perhaps even spending the winter in a warm place such as Florida or Arizona.

A half century later, this scenario is about as dated as the brand-new-at-the-time inventions of touch-tone phones and cassette tapes. Today, for many reasons, "unretirement" is a far more viable template of living for older Americans than retirement, making it a guiding force for baby boomers as they plunge headlong into their sixties and seventies. Even before Chris Farrell popularized the term with his 2014 book of that name, unretirement was offering many boomers an appealing alternative to the standard one-day-working-and-the-next-day-not-working model that was in place for those around age 65. Farrell pushed the concept further, however, arguing that it was in boomers' best interests to develop skills that would prove useful in generating income significantly beyond than the usual age of retirement. Working well into one's sixties or longer, even on a part-time basis, would make a huge difference versus relying solely on savings, assuming one had any. Waiting as long as possible to tap into one's nest egg was a smart investment strategy, Farrell made clear, urging boomers to begin thinking about their financial future as soon as possible. An income stream would also allow those in their early sixties to wait to claim Social Security benefits until they were 66 or 70, another smart financial move.[1] In Reboot terms, boomers who were not independently wealthy had better ponder how to reinvent themselves professionally, he posited, with the notion of unretirement far more sustainable than retirement.

The trick, of course, is figuring out what to do after one's first career has run its course. For most, how to translate one's skills into something new is the key, unless one would be content making minimum wage and possibly tips. About half of the baristas at my local Starbucks appear to be in their sixties, in fact, as are many workers in general in the food service and hospitality business. I know someone who left the prestigious managerial position he had held for 30 years at Standard & Poor's, the financial services and ratings agency, and is now cutting cheese at a Whole Foods (quite happily, I must add). After being a lawyer and then chief counsel at a large company for more than 20 years, a mid-fifties friend I know came into work one day and was promptly fired, completely out of the blue. He was in the fortunate position to have enough financial resources for the rest of life but for him, like many boomers, time rather than money was the critical issue. The current actuarial table says that this person will live another 25 years or so, a lot of time to fill doing the puzzle page in the newspaper. After considering his options, he and his wife have opened up a spin cycle studio in their hometown, a perfect example of how many boomers are rebooting out of necessity or choice.

Perhaps the best news about the emergence of unretirement is that most boomers want to keep working as long as possible. Seventy-two percent of those aged 50 or older said exactly that in a 2014 survey conducted by Merrill Lynch and the consulting firm Age Wave, something that bodes well for boomers' financial future as well as that of the country as a whole.[2] As long as there are jobs to fill or create—a big if, admittedly—the economic and health care train wreck and generational war that many are predicting for the country due to the hordes of boomers demanding their entitlements is unwarranted. There is no doubt that a significant portion of boomers have not saved enough to live out their later years in comfort, meaning that it's essential that Social Security and Medicare survive.

Unretirement is clearly a buffer against such a nightmare scenario, however, promising to turn boomers from an economic liability into a valuable asset. Well-educated, relatively healthy, and eager to work, boomers are from a human resources perspective excellent potential employees, with only ageism standing in the way of giving them the jobs they want, deserve, and are perfectly capable of doing. Sixty- and 70-somethings may not have been able to do the kind of work required before Social Security was passed in 1935, but many of those of today are, particularly because so many jobs today involve looking at a computer versus standing on a factory floor. Finally, because interaction with other people is key to living longer, healthier lives, a robust job market for boomers would actually save the country billions in health care costs, another good reason to hope that unretirement gains traction in the years ahead.

OPPORTUNITY

View boomers' third act through the lens of unretirement versus retirement.

ENCORE CAREERS

With unretirement as the backdrop, many baby boomers are embarking on second or "encore" careers after their original one, marking a major and perhaps even historic transformation of the workplace. After putting in 30 or 35 years at a job, some are calling it quits or, like my friend, told not to bother coming in the following morning. City, state, and federal employees, like military personnel, public school teachers, police, fire-fighters, and garbage collectors have often earned full retirement benefits by age 60, but many are not content waiting for their pension check to arrive in the mail. Retirees of the last generation or two may have been happy to celebrate their last day or work and sail off into the sunset, but most baby boomers have no intention of ending the productive phase of their lives. Fifty-nine percent fully employed people in their fifties and 82 percent in their early sixties say they will still be working after reaching age 65 and may not retire at all, the Transamerica Center for Retirement Studies reported, meaning encore careers will play an important role in boomers' third acts.[3]

Encore careers can mean staying at the company at which one already works but in a redefined role. While widespread ageism in the workplace is a pernicious issue that often goes unreported, there are signs that more companies are beginning to appreciate the worth of older employees and are putting into place policies in order to keep them. Abbot, Lancaster Labs, and Hewlett Packard offer workday flexibility (fewer hours, position sharing, staged retirement, or part-time jobs), for example, while Volkswagen of America and Mercy Health Systems are taking related steps (flexible schedules, yearly hours, or a "squeezed" week of work). Dow Chemical Company, Duke Power, and CNA Insurance are companies offering career elasticity (start/stop opportunities, "timeouts," fewer responsibilities, position reassignments, and gradual retirements), while Quest Diagnostics, IBM, the U.S. Federal Government, CVS/Caremark Pharmacies, Carondelet Health Network, and Home Depot are providing location flexibility (remote employment, work from multiple places, or "snow birding"). Finally, companies such as Polaroid, MIT, The Aerospace Corporation, Busch Entertainment, SC Johnson, Principal Financial Group, and Hoffman-LaRoche are showing more tolerance in the employer-employee relationship itself (project assignments, consulting opportunities, and part-time work), and Mitretek, First Horizon National, Baptist Health Systems, and Lincoln Financial Services are doing interesting things with benefits (meal plans and retirement perks). Organizations such as these have a clear understanding of boomers' long-term career plans that require some flexibility, hopefully the harbinger of an emerging, more accommodating workplace.[4]

By offering education and training to baby boomers to help them reinvent themselves, Encore.org is helping to advance the encore career marketplace while also serving social ends. Founded in 1997 by Marc Freedman as Civic Ventures, Encore.org has vigorously promoted the idea of encore careers, in the process growing on a parallel path with the aging of boomers. With their idealist roots, it's not surprising that many boomers are wishing to reboot by finding socially meaningful work. As Chapter 9 will show, boomers are actively engaged in the pursuit to "pay it forward," that is, to give back to society in gratitude for the rewards they reaped via their first careers. Encore.org works with colleges and universities to develop programs that will enable boomers to find positions for the "greater good," a noble effort by any measure. Getting paid for work that combines one's personal passion with a social purpose (often in health care, education, or government) is an incredibly powerful proposition that Encore.org is making real. Again, community colleges in particular have positioned themselves as excellent resources for delivering knowledge that is not just relevant but could be tailored to meet the requirements of older learners. The nonprofit's Encore U, meanwhile, focuses on programs at four-year colleges and universities, with business schools at University of Washington, Tulane University, Princeton University, Portland State University, Stanford University, and Harvard University signing up.[5]

AARP too is providing resources for boomers to forge encore careers either at a nonprofit or through a Fortune 500 "transition program." AARP. org's Second Career section offers advice, online job search sites, and fascinating mini case histories of boomers who successfully made the leap from a traditional job into an encore career. At 61, for example, systems engineer Keith Gordon became a high school math teacher through IBM's "Transition to Teaching" program, while at age 57 Beverly Robinson rebooted herself from a college provost to a goat farmer via a government technical assistance program. Sixty-seven-year-old Kate Young, meanwhile, recast herself from the director of a nonprofit to a sustainable agricultural specialist through a Peace Corps program, and 59-year-old Noel Durrant from a quality and reliability program manager to a technology educator via an Intel Encore Fellowship.[6] Such cheerful stories provide firm evidence that encore careers for boomers are entirely possible, a very good thing for everyone.

OPPORTUNITY

Make your company an agent of encore careers.

ONLINE DATING

The last time many boomers tried to pursue some version of romance was in a Jimmy Carter-era fern bar or disco and when "What's Your Sign?" was asked non-ironically. Just like millennials, however, boomers today are going online to find that special or reasonably likeable person, a much more efficient means of starting a new relationship.

One in eight of all American boomers are using online dating websites, a 2015 Pew Research survey found, an impressive figure that indicates that the group is rebooting their personal lives as well as their professional ones.[7] Fee-based Match.com is the biggest such site, but there are many free ones catering to single (or perhaps not so much) boomers such as Plenty of Fish (POF). Facebook and Meetup are other sites for boomers to look for love or an approximate facsimile, as those are well suited for users to find others who share a common interest.

Internet-savvy boomers search for a mate just as they might for a good stock—measuring likely future performance based on relevant metrics and past history. Much of job searching too has shifted online, of course, making the screening of and pitch to a particular person a familiar process. Online shopping, in which one scrutinizes everything in a category on a site like Amazon rather than hope to find what one wants among the things that are on display at a mall, is another useful analogy to explain the popularity of online dating. Expectedly, newly divorced and recently widowed boomers account for a significant percentage of online daters. In fact, the "gray" divorce percentage has jumped significantly in recent years; only 1 in 10 people over the age of 50 got divorced in 1990, but about 1 in 4 did in 2009, a team of Bowling Green State University sociologists found. Also, one out of every three unmarried boomers has always been single, that university's National Center for Family and Marriage Research reported in 2012, making these folks also prime candidates for online dating.[8] Single empty nesters who suddenly find themselves with a lot of time (and a lonely house) on their hands represent one more sizable segment, making it understandable why online dating among boomers has become a kind of cultural phenomenon. Grown children of boomers are sometimes concerned or uncomfortable seeing their mom or dad cruising

Tinder or OKCupid to get together with someone, even sometimes giving them the be-sure-to-practice-safe-sex talk before going out on a date.

Another site, the unfortunately named Coffee Meets Bagel, is experiencing especially high growth (81% in 2014 and 314% in 2015) among 55–64-year-olds. Women tend to be especially enthusiastic users of this and online dating sites in general, perhaps because they are more likely to be single in their later years because of the death of their husband. (In 2012, the life expectancy for American women was 81.2 years while that for men was 76.4 years.)[9] Dating among boomers dispels many of the myths surrounding romance in one's third act of life. "By and large this age group is happier, more secure, and even feeling sexier than their younger counterparts," noted Dr. Terri Orbuch, relationship expert for the 50+ dating site Ourtime.com, thinking that boomers are also "better judges of the type of person who will make them happy." Besides having greater life experience, the fact is that boomers likely have fewer years ahead of them than younger people, something that makes them want to use their time wisely, especially that spent with a potential partner.[10]

With 30 percent of boomers now being single, it's no wonder that marketers are going after the group with more and more online dating sites. IAC, which owns sites like Match.com and Chemistry.com, started Ourtime.com in 2011 for 50-and-over singles looking to date, and in April 2014, Stitch.net, a Tinder-like dating app for the over-50 set, was launched. Like Tinder, it shows users just one profile at a time, and it alerts them to profiles where a person they've liked has liked them back, so they're less likely to contact someone and get no response. Stitch also does extensive background checks, a good thing given all the Internet trollers looking for something other than love or companionship.[11]

While some online dating sites for younger people may be mostly about hooking up, those for older folks like Stitch are serving a greater purpose. "Our grand vision is to help improve the lives of older adults in every country around the world by addressing the many causes of social isolation and loneliness," say the founders of Stitch, recognizing they are solving a serious problem while also running a for-profit business. More boomers are finding themselves alone after having a partner for decades and, for a variety of good reasons, have not had success meeting another soulmate. Many people on Stitch start out as pen pals in what is a safe environment, happy to communicate for weeks, months, or even years before getting together in person. Building a friendship first is often a good foundation for a romantic relationship, experts point out, making Stitch and others like it much more than your typical online dating site. "We thank you all for whatever algorithm you have in place that matched us," say Stitch users Nancy and Bob, obviously two happy customers.[12]

HIPSTERVILLES

Spoiler alert for Sun City and other retirement communities that used to define the good life for older Americans: baby boomers want to live among people of all ages and cultural orientations rather than just people who look and act a lot like themselves. Because they do not resemble real life (and are decidedly uncool), communities restricted to those 55+ and designed for "active senior living" do not fit very well into most boomers' plans for their act. Boomers love authenticity, diversity, and energy, and are thus choosing places to live that incorporate those values. In addition, the idea of sorting communities into buckets defined by age, that is, "young," "middle-aged," and "old," has, like Elvis, left the building. No one, especially your typical baby boomer, suddenly gets "old" when he or she turns a certain age, making any product or service purposely conceived to fit the wants or needs of an older consumer probably a bad idea.

One might not think hipster neighborhoods would be a destination of choice for people who were eligible to vote in the 1968 presidential election, for example, but such is the case. With cash in hand, boomers are moving into trendy urban neighborhoods like Williamsburg in Brooklyn, attracted to the place for the same, simple reason many 20-somethings love it for—it's interesting and inspiring. Developers of high-rise, high-end condos in that part of New York City have been somewhat surprised that not every buyer is a millennial making big bucks or with a fat bank account courtesy of mommy or daddy. Rather, it's mommy and/or daddy herself or himself who wants it, with these 50- or 60-somethings elated to live somewhere that exudes such *joie de vivre*. Many of these boomers are relocating from the family-friendly suburbs, finding hipstervilles to be a wonderful change of place from the house and town that served them very well while they were raising kids. Uber-cool downtown Seattle, artsy LoHi (Lower Highlands) in Denver, and the Rittenhouse Square area of

Philadelphia are also experiencing an influx of boomers, making savvy developers like Toll Brothers take note and create a "city living" division. Younger homeowners may not be particularly happy about people who look disturbingly like their mom or dad establishing digs in their hood but should find consolation in the fact that their apartment is probably now worth a lot more money.[13]

College towns may not be particularly hip, but they too offer boomers the chance to be reinspired. With loads of young, mostly enthusiastic people looking forward rather than backward, such towns also represent a more sanguine alternative to a traditional retirement community. There's a palpable sense of energy on and around college campuses, with the always exciting aura of learning in the air. Boomers are returning to such communities for the intellectual stimulation and cultural amenities, especially those in which they lived 40 or 50 years ago when they were students. As Chapter 2 showed, boomers view learning as a lifelong pursuit, making it perfectly sensible that they would choose to live in a college town in their older years. Fully aware of this, college and university officials are encouraging local residents over 55 to take free or low-cost classes, knowing an educated public is a cornerstone of a healthy, vibrant community. Regular sporting events, concerts, and lectures are other good reasons why boomers (or anyone else) should consider a college town to put down roots. If that weren't enough, many such towns offer good health care, affordable housing, and happen to be located in states with low tax rates for those possessing financial assets but not bringing in much income.[14]

For those with a passion for food and football, especially when combined as tailgating, there may not be a better college town than Oxford, Mississippi. Home to Ole Miss, Oxford also has a distinct literary atmosphere by the presence of John Grisham, Square Books (a great indie bookstore), and the ghost of William Faulkner, who produced his best work there. Oxford is also attractive because of its low property taxes and comparatively cheap cost of living, and each semester one university course is offered gratis to those who are no longer working full time. The winters in Ann Arbor, Michigan, are abysmal, but that isn't stopping more hearty boomers from establishing residence there. That town's Osher Lifelong Learning Institute is one of the growing numbers of educational programs that are designed specifically for older adults, offering noncredit but university-level courses in the arts and humanities.[15]

Music and art lovers, meanwhile, may opt for Austin, Texas, when choosing where to put down stakes. Any number of good bands can be seen on any given night and, fittingly with the state's obsession with size, the Blanton Museum of Art at the University of Texas has the country's biggest university-owned collection on exhibit. University associations in Austin invest or co-invest in developing residences for alumni, such as Longhorn Village, where residents can use the campus library, receive discounts on social events, and audit classes. There are many other great college towns for boomers but none brainier (and more walkable, increasing the feeling of connectness) than Cambridge, Massachusetts, home to both Harvard and MIT.[16]

OPPORTUNITY

Locate more educated and affluent boomers in hipster neighborhoods and college towns.

WELLNESS TRAVEL

They were the generation that defined health and fitness, leading the jogging trend in the 1970s, the aerobics trend of the 1980s, and the yoga trend of the 1990s, all the while shunning artificial colors and flavors in the name of naturalness. The spike in Americans regularly exercising showed up in the numbers—lower cholesterol, blood pressure levels, and deaths from heart disease, and longer average life expectancies. The self-help and New Age movements of these same decades helped to make working out not just a physical activity but a kind of spiritual experience, conveying the message that to love one's body was to love oneself. Exercise videos sold like hotcakes, and gyms became "health clubs," with members joining up for its social scene as much as its fitness equipment. Fitness and fashion coalesced with leotards, Lycra, and leg warmers, and icons of health like Jane Fonda, Arnold Schwarzenegger, and Richard Simmons (really?) were celebrated in pop culture. Having a personal trainer became somewhat of a status symbol, and completing a marathon (or, better yet, a triathlon) earned big bragging rights around the water cooler. The Presidential Physical Fitness programs of the mid-1960s likely laid the foundation for all this to come, pushing 10-year-old boomers like myself to do as many push-ups, chin-ups, and jumping jacks as possible in order to create a healthier nation during the Cold War.[17]

"Then something strange happened," wrote Sarah Mahoney in *AARP: The Magazine* in 2014, observing that "boomers, once the peppiest generation, devolved from fit to flabby." Indeed, contrary to popular belief, boomers' collective health and fitness is today not a pretty picture. High blood pressure and diabetes are facts of life for many, with fast food, our online lifestyle, and mantra that time is money are a few factors that helped to bring on this sad state of affairs. Aging bodies is of course the biggest culprit, as slower metabolism leads to weight gain and many other health issues.[18] And after feeling a little too much burn or pumping too much iron, knee and joint replacements have become commonplace among boomers, another part of what many justifiably believe is a real crisis among the once healthiest generation in history. The abysmal health care industry in this country is another barrier to the kind of preventive medicine that we all should practice. Copays, should one be lucky enough to have health insurance, continue to skyrocket, making one put off going to a doctor for as long as possible.

Told by their doctor (or spouse) they better shape up or else, however, many boomers are rebooting their bodies by recommitting to some kind of health and fitness regime. A major health scare or just too long of a look in the mirror also can lead to the sudden realization that not just appearance but both quality and quantity of life are at stake. Americans are living longer, but with that comes the greater chance that one will develop at least one chronic condition at some point—the devil's bargain we have made with increased longevity. Doing the usual things—eating well and usually less, exercising daily, and cutting out the standard vices—is the first step in staying healthy, but some boomers are taking more active steps to achieve a physical and mental sense of well-being. Spas have been around for a long time, of course, but now wellness travel has emerged as a prime way to reboot aging bodies. Wellness travel is a multibillion-dollar industry in which people use a vacation to maintain, promote, or kick-start a healthy way of living. Losing weight or getting fitter are the most common goals, but other aspects of wellness—managing stress, reconnecting with oneself or a significant other, or communing with nature—are also often part of this kind of travel. Getting a good massage at a luxurious spa is all fine and good, but wellness travel is about learning how to eat better, sleep better, and exercise better in order to prevent or at least delay the onset of disease.[19]

No marketer more than InterContinental Hotel Group's EVEN Hotels understands the opportunity that wellness travel presents. "We provide a strong lifestyle offering for travellers seeking more options to stay healthier and happier away from home," EVEN tells visitors to its website, promising to offer guests "a best-in-class fitness experience, healthier food choices and natural, relaxing spaces." The 202-room flagship EVEN Hotels Brooklyn, which is the brand's fourth hotel and second in New York City, was clearly conceived with wellness in mind, that is, designed to help guests "eat well, rest easy, keep active, and accomplish more." EVEN has carved out space in the hotel industry as the only holistic wellness brand and is committed to providing a form of personalized service in which the staff encourage guests to take a wellness philosophy back home with them. In addition to the hotel's Cork & Kale Market and Bar (named after their customizable signature black kale salad) and eye-popping Athletic Studio, classes in yoga and spinning can be enjoyed, not to mention group runs to Brooklyn Bridge Park with the hotel's CWO (Chief Wellness Officer) leading the way.[20] At the forefront of wellness travel, EVEN is doing nothing less than revolutionizing the hotel experience, a breath of fresh air in what is for the most part a stale and musty industry.

OPPORTUNITY

Offer palatable ways for boomers to achieve wellness.

SPIRITUAL RETREATS

A wholesale return to traditional religion among baby boomers as they get older, as some experts are predicting?[21] Unlikely. Generations past got the old-time religion as they aged, a function of facing a serious illness, losing a loved one, or confronting one's own mortality. But boomers have never followed the pattern of previous generations, especially when large, powerful institutions are involved. Since they were teenagers, boomers have viewed both church and state with considerable suspicion, questioning whose interests were being served as figures of authority dictated what one could and should do. Traditional Judeo-Christianity still does not fit the spiritual needs or interests of many boomers particularly well, suggesting that religion in America will continue to decline as it has for the past half century.

That hardly means that boomers' spiritual sides are ebbing, however. In fact, there are definite signs that boomers are increasingly interested in matters of faith as they search for greater meaning and purpose in their lives. Boomers were justifiably notorious for living in the material world in the 1980s and 1990s as they freely and unapologetically engaged in conspicuous consumption, but now a good many are trying to figure out how to become more complete human beings. Doing that requires an existential rebooting of sorts by making a concerted effort to find possible answers to the big questions of life. While more than 85 percent of Americans believe in some kind of divine power, just around 30 percent of that group regularly goes to a religious service, according to the Baylor Longitudinal Study of Religion.[22] Likewise, many boomers are foregoing traditional religion but engaging in a nearly infinite variety of personal expressions of spirituality. Self-help, New Age, and Oprah each heavily informed boomers' spiritual sensibility, taking them to a place where they are ready to dive headfirst into the juicy areas of enrichment, discovery, and personal growth.

"Self-discovery" trips are nothing new, as Roger Sands of usnews .com recently reported, but baby boomers asking the big questions of life are turning them into a major chunk of the travel industry. Spirituality rebooters are going anywhere and everywhere on meditative retreats, which typically revolve around travelers seeking ways to become enlightened people with a greater understanding of their own purpose in life. Because there is no single path to self-discovery, those in the hospitality biz are offering all kinds of programs intended to heighten wanderers' perception of themselves and their relative sense of well-being. The journey each individual takes is a lot less important than the final destination, allowing marketers in this segment to tap into a wide range of physical, emotional, and even romantic activities that may lead travelers to the inner peace that they are searching for.[23]

More inquisitive boomers are, for example, embarking on inward journeys at The Lodge at Woodloch in Hawley, Pennsylvania, which is much more than a luxurious spa. The Lodge promotes a "personal awakening philosophy," providing guests with the all-too-rare chance to escape their ordinary selves and examine their existence in relation to the universe. The Lodge's "Journaling for Self-Discovery" class, for example, instructs guests in the fundamentals of keeping a journal via directed self-analysis steeped in emotional sensations. Country Walkers based in Williston, Vermont, meanwhile, offers 21st-century pilgrims a self-guided walking adventure tour in some of the most beautiful places on the planet. Discovering the world on foot helps to put one's life in context, many find, especially if one is lucky enough to walk an ancient trail in Tuscany in Italy.

The local cuisine is a religious experience in itself and staying at converted monasteries in Pienza and Siena add to the feeling that time and space no longer exist.[24]

For a quicker and closer spiritual reboot, New Yorkers are heading to The Mayflower Grace in Washington, Connecticut, well known as a prime destination for meditation. "There's a newfound interest in meditation getaways among the general population—especially baby boomers, who grew up in the '60s and already have a certain familiarity with the precepts of Eastern spiritualism," noted Sarah Gold in explaining the popularity of places like The Mayflower Grace. The retreat offers guests "Sound Healing," which uses the heavenly audible resonance of a Tibetan Bowl, prompting a soothing and regenerative sense of well-being. While tilting decidedly toward the more woo-woo side, Sound Healing is said to be capable of leading the physical self into a state of homeostasis, which even many Western physicians believe is the ideal condition for the body to heal itself.[25]

Finally, at The Chopra Center for Wellbeing in Carlsbad, California, healing specialists assist guests to realize greater mind-body-spirit balance. Established by superstar holistic doctors Deepak Chopra and David Simon, the center has for more than 20 years been somewhere in which individuals have gone to become healthier, happier, and more fulfilled people. Best of all, the center integrates what it calls "the healing arts of the East with the best in modern Western medicine," the right approach for those wanting to reboot their spiritual and physical selves.[26]

OPPORTUNITY

Ride along with boomers on their spiritual journey.

FOUR

Inner Muse

Envision a world where all individuals flourish across their lifespan through creative expression.

Vision of the National Center for Creative Aging

A decade or so ago, two college friends, Alex Farkas and Stephen Tanenbaum, cofounded Ugallery, an online art gallery. Initially, the pair specialized in the work of young artists and targeted young art buyers as their primary market. Over the last 10 years, however, the company has shifted both its mix of artists and its target market. Of the more than 500 artists the gallery represents, the majority is older than 50 and one-fourth are at least 60. "We have seen an evolution of our artist roster become more of the older demographic, as well as some of the customers," Tanenbaum said in explaining his company's change of direction. "Art is a great way for baby boomers to enrich their lives at the next stage," he added, hitting the nail on the head.[1]

As this slice of life suggests, there is an intimate relationship between baby boomers and creativity, one that will no doubt continue to blossom. Research shows that creativity helps mid-lifers and older people stay engaged and feel good about themselves and serves as a prime way for them to remain optimistic and excited about life.[2] Fortunately, boomers have been steeped in creativity throughout their lives, with aesthetics viewed as an essential way to express one's individuality. Given all this, finding one's inner muse—the goddess of art—will be a primary pursuit of boomers in their third act, I believe, particularly because they will have more time and money to nurture a particular avenue of creativity. Partnering with boomers as they court their personal muse thus makes a lot of sense for many companies, as creativity has been proven to be a genuine fountain of youth.

History is certainly on baby boomers' side when considering the role that creativity will play in their lives in the years and decades ahead. Creative geniuses ranging from Frank Lloyd Wright to George Burns worked well into their nineties, proof positive that, contrary to popular belief, the brain cells of cognitively healthy individuals do not stop regenerating. This will be especially true for boomers because their roots of creativity run so deep. Author Brant Green suggests that boomers' coming of age in the 1960s and 1970s served as the foundation for their lifelong love of creativity. During those two seminal decades, creativity was "the fuel of the cultural engine," Green wrote in his 2006 *Marketing to Leading-Edge Baby Boomers*, whether expressed through rock 'n' roll lyrics and album covers, Broadway shows like *Jesus Christ Superstar* and *Hair*, pop art, writing by the likes of Hunter Thompson, Ken Kesey, and Kurt Vonnegut, auteur filmmaking, or fashion seemingly inspired by the hallucinogenic recreational activities of the times. Photography, sculpture, dance, and silk screening (as well as candle making and leather clothing design, unfortunately) became popular pastimes, permanently encoding creativity into boomers' DNA.[3] A half century later, baby boomers' love affair with creativity remains strong, meaning there will be much courting of one's inner muse to come.

OPPORTUNITY

Surf the wave of boomer creativity as they age.

CREATIVE AGING

For a few decades now, the concept of creative aging has been on the same upward trajectory as the graying of America. Creative aging is "the practice of engaging older adults (55+) in participatory, professionally run arts programs with a focus on social engagement and skills mastery," according to the nonprofit organization Lifetime Arts, making it clear that "it is not about making macaroni necklaces." With millions of baby boomers entering their third act of life, creative aging has grown into a full-scale movement designed to provide opportunities for creatively expressing oneself in a meaningful way via artistic get-togethers. On a grander level, creative aging is about possibilities, adds Pat Spadafora of the Sheridan Centre for Elder Research, and "freeing ourselves of limiting beliefs about aging and embracing the reality that individuals continue to grow, learn, and contribute to their communities throughout the life journey."[4]

With such a positive approach to the reality that we all get older (a rare thing, strangely enough), it's not surprising that creative aging has become a major force to be reckoned with. Through its research, public policy, professional development, and formation of hundreds of arts programs, the National Center for Creative Aging (NCCA) is without a doubt the biggest champion of the movement. Art-related pursuits are vital to helping older people remain dynamic members of society and an important part of their communities, the NCCA reasonably suggests. Community-based arts programming also is helpful for young people in that it sends a powerful, positive message, the NCCA has found in its research, meaning creative aging is a good thing for everyone on a local and national level.[5]

Creative aging also has much to do with health. Wellness can be realized in a wide variety of ways, one of which is employing creativity to exercise the mind, body, and spirit. Research has shown that older people who regularly take part in artistic endeavors go to the doctor less and need to take fewer medications versus people who do not express their creativity. "There is a growing body of evidence indicating that creative programs for older adults improve the health and wellness of older adults, as well as encourage social connectivity," said Dr. Marc Agronin, adult and geriatric psychiatrist for the Miami Jewish Health Systems (MJHS), the biggest long-term health care facility in Florida. Studies show that cognition kindled by artistic pursuits can be particularly therapeutic for those with thinking and memory problems. Also, it has been proven that creativity improves the relationships between people with mental challenges and anyone who provides them with care.[6] The chances of becoming a victim of dementia or Alzheimer's disease become greater as one gets older, meaning the graying of America and the world will bring about more such cases. It's thus difficult to overestimate the potential impact of making possible creativity-based activities to those with mental challenges now and especially in the future.

The number and range of creative aging programs in the United States is truly remarkable, in part due to generous funding from the MetLife Foundation. (Go to creativeaging.org/programs for the full list.) Intergenerational activities take place in all kinds of geographic areas and in many different places in which older people tend to congregate. At Creative Aging Cincinnati, for example, folks can take part in different forms of dance and "creative movement," something called "chair yoga," drum circles, music making, and art classes. In Fairfax, Virginia, the Potomac Arts Academy provides piano lessons for 55+ers with no previous musical background. Students meet with teachers weekly over the course of a couple of months, after which there is a relaxed recital for friends and family members. And at the Arts & Minds program offered by the New York Historical Society and the Studio Museum in Harlem, individuals who have cognitive issues along with their caregivers meet to engage in different kinds of creative experiences. A diverse set of artistic activities created with such people in mind can be had as well as classes for educators and caregivers. Following collaborative dialogues that focus on different artistic genres, students get to make their own art, with each workshop supervised by an expert in the field.[7] Such programs may deem geezery, but it's important to keep in mind that the leading wave of boomers are already in their seventies and, needless to say, not getting any younger.

The NCCA tree branches out into other creativity-oriented initiatives targeted to 55+ers. With its Beautiful Minds project cosponsored by DSM Nutritional Products, for example, creative agers are invited to take part in a nationwide photography exhibit featuring individuals able to see "beautiful things" all around them regardless of their age. The exhibit travels across the country to encourage everyone to maintain his or her brain health through artistic pursuits. Beautiful Minds is dedicated to "improving brain health in all stages of life by providing research, education, and inspiring stories," the NCCA declares, a beautiful thing in itself that other organizations marketing products or services to boomers can learn from.[8]

OPPORTUNITY

Support creative aging as boomers rush headlong into their seventies and eighties.

VISUAL ARTISTS

While creative aging is more about well-being than anything else, more baby boomers are taking the leap of making art their new careers. After retiring from their traditional careers as stockbrokers, doctors, techies, small business owners, or whatever else served them well for decades, these 60-somethings are creating and selling things of their own design. Fortunately, the brains of such folks are working in their favor. While older brains may have slowed down a bit, they are actually better than young ones in using the left and right hemispheres in harmony. Younger peoples' brains tend to compartmentalize the two sides of the brain, in other words, whereas with older people the barriers between them lessen and enable verbal/nonverbal and logical/emotional processing to more fully mingle. In addition, empty nesters usually have more time to do what they want, this too accounting for the flourishing of boomer creativity.[9]

Real-life stories about baby boomers wooing their inner muse are indeed impressive. Bill Sanders of Steamboat Springs, Colorado, for example, sold his lumber and wood flooring business to become a ceramics artist, finding significantly more happiness in making dishware and decorative pots than worrying if a shipment of engineered hardwood arrived. Jennifer O'Day of Austin, Texas, meanwhile, decided to stop trading stocks in order to pursue her calling of mixed-media artwork, finding the latter to be a more enriching experience. And when Geri deGruy found her career as a therapist too emotionally grueling (many of her clients were abused women), she chose textile arts as the way to spend her time. Each of these people, who had happily built up a nest egg before they made their move, reports that all of their senses seemed to come alive when they became artists. "It really sharpens my ability to see visually and perceptively and I think tactilely," O'Day stated, seeing creativity as something that "engages the whole mind-body-soul." The feeling that life is short so you better do what you love was another common theme among those who became artists in their third act, something all of us might keep in mind as we chart our own life course.[10]

Displaced workers from the technology industry seem to be especially prone toward turning to their inner muse. With few exceptions, anyone older than 50 is considered well past his or her prime in tech culture, and younger employees freely admit they are uncomfortable working with someone who could be the age of their mom or dad. Many mid-life geeks who survived the dot-com bubble but now find themselves unwelcome in Silicon Valley are exploring their creative sides, especially those who were the beneficiaries of large windfalls when they left their respective companies. Interestingly, those with a mechanical engineering or software background find certain arts, such as jewelry or metal making, a natural transition, as each field relies on technical skills in creating something.[11]

If you have any doubts about the creative aspirations of baby boomers, all you need to do is check out boomerinas.com, whose wry mission is to "help baby boomer women find their footing, find their voices, and find fashion that fits." "Boomerinas are grown-up little girls who wanted to be ballerinas, rock stars, novelists, fashion models, designers, princesses, and a lot of other grand things," the website states, "and, even though we may not have fulfilled all of our dreams, there is still time to reawaken that inspiration from long ago."[12]

Featured on boomerinas.com is folk artist Marti Sullan, a classic boomerina whose story exemplifies boomer creativity. As a child of the 1950s, Sullan grew up in a Cape Cod-style house (with an original price tag of $5,000!) in a suburban neighborhood where the moms were housewives and the kids created their own fun. While wandering in the nearby woods was a frequent pastime, Sullan's mother (an avid reader and writer) provided her with plenty of art supplies—construction paper, crayons, and watercolors—for drawing and painting. Her dad, meanwhile, an accountant (and part-time jazz musician), brought home boxes of paper that had printing on one side but was blank on the other. With free, unlimited paper and encouragement from her parents to use it any way she wanted, Sullan's artistic imagination was free to run wild.[13]

With the great outdoors just a short distance from her house, Sullan drew picture after picture of animals, fish, and flowers, focusing on the details of, say, a particular weed or caterpillar. "I examined everything closely and retained those images, and that is why I could draw well at an early age," she recalled, remembering that in first grade she got an award for a poster of an owl she made. Adults were amazed at how lifelike the drawing was but she wasn't, finding the process quite easy. With the arts well funded during the 1960s, there were plenty of art classes to take in junior high school and high school that were taught by teachers who encouraged her creativity. Marriage and kids sidelined her inner muse for a few decades, but she recently returned to her creative roots and, at age 61, was excited to be teaching art classes to young people and adults.[14] Sullan's story is not that unusual and speaks of the renaissance of creativity among millions of baby boomers.

OPPORTUNITY

Feature boomer artists in your advertising.

BLOGGING

For those who have the time and something to say, blogging is nothing less than a godsend. As online journals, blogs are an ideal vehicle to share one's thoughts on any and every subject imaginable and potentially reach thousands of readers. Blogs are steeped in personal passions, making them a goldmine for marketers wishing to gain a deeper understanding of what any particular community of people cares deeply about. Boomer blogs represent a subculture all their own, as folks exploring their inner muse detail the good, bad, and ugly of aging. There is no shortage of blogs and websites written by boomers for boomers, including Baby Boomer Headquarters, Baby Boomer Magazine, Boomers Life, Baby Boomer News, Boomer Times, Life after Fifty, Boomer Authority, Baby Boomers Social Club, Everything Zoomer, Fab over Fifty, The Second Half, Baby Boomer Daily, Boomer Girl Diary, Rock the Wrinkle, The Booming Life, and, last but not least, The Fabulous Geezersisters.

Standing out from the crowd, however, is The Huffington Post's blog dedicated to baby boomers and their Post 50. Bloggers who express their inner muse for Huff Post Baby Boomers cover the usual journalistic beat centered on lifestyle, that is, home, fashion, health, and the arts. But the blog also digs deep into boomer culture, tackling subjects that are indigenous to the group. (Recent posts include "10 Sure Signs You Were Born in the 1950s," "The Midlife Crisis: A Misleading Myth or a Reality in Search of a New Name," and "4 Big Parenting Mistakes Boomers Have Made.") Post 50 is even more boomer-centric, with its blog posts focused on reinvention, retirement, "voices of strength," and Alzheimer's awareness. AARP-like topics like rekindling romance, fighting ageism, dealing with the physicality of getting older, and staying happy make up Post 50, offering a wide-open window into the everyday lives of baby boomers.[15]

Boomer Café and Next Avenue are two other blog sites that are doing a good job in talking to boomers about issues they find relevant. While leaning a little too much toward nostalgia (do we really need one more list of the best songs of the 1960s or 1970s?), Boomer Café ("the original digital magazine for baby boomers with active lifestyles and youthful spirits") does to its credit have a whole section on "Money & Work." Advice for boomers on finding a job, working from home, finding the best freebies, combating ageism in the workplace, and changing one's life can be found amidst the many stories steeped in memory.[16] Next Avenue ("where grown-ups keep growing") sorts its blogs into five sections to which virtually all boomers can relate: "Health & Well-Being," "Money & Security," "Work & Purpose," "Living & Learning," and "Caregiving." With many boomers having to look after their elderly parents, Next Avenue's Caregiving section is especially valuable. Bloggers with experience in this very tough part of life discuss finding and selecting care and housing, providing support to caregivers, dealing with dying and death, and thinking both financial and legally. There is also a list of services and resources that many will no doubt find very useful.[17]

Some boomers are building businesses around their blogs, making an opportunity for themselves to generate some cash. Elaine Ambrose of Eagle, Idaho, for example, has had her amusing blog syndicated and it now generates hundreds of thousands of hits on Huffington Post, for example; she has also started a related venture that publishes the work of lesser-known writers and gives away the royalties to worthy causes.[18] Joan Price, meanwhile, has carved out an interesting niche with her Better Than I Ever Expected blog. Price is a leading "sexpert" who celebrates the joys and addresses the challenges of senior sex, a topic that many younger people consider to be disturbing (or even oxymoronic). (Old folks' homes are actually hotbeds of sexuality.) Better Than I Ever Expected is sensibly targeted to "sex-positive" boomers and older people, with her various books (including *Naked at Our Age* and *The Ultimate Guide to Sex After 50*) available there as well.[19] Boomers led the sexual revolution, of course, making businesses like that of Price seem to be in the right place at the right time.

Not surprisingly, travel comprises a big chunk of boomer blogs. The Roaming Boomers, which is part of a full service travel agency of that same name, is one of the best. On the site, which is run by a married couple who dropped out of the corporate world to pursue their own passion of travel, there are over 1,000 articles detailing a particular destination they visited. Roaming Boomers helps its wanderlusters plan their trips over sea and land, whether solo or in groups. The company cleverly uses its blog as a teaser, making nearly any reader just want to pick up and go. One recent blog post featured the couple's visit to the Margerie Glacier in Alaska, a piece of ice over a mile wide and about 25 stories over the water. After reading such an article and seeing the accompanying photos and videos, visitors to the site want to become roaming boomers themselves, precisely the point. Roaming Boomers claims to be the preeminent online resource for luxury boomer travelers, a good example of how blogging can be the seed for fruitful enterprises.[20]

OPPORTUNITY

Incorporate boomer blogging on your website to extend
your relationship with the group.

CREATIVE ENTREPRENEURSHIP

In 2007, Facebook CEO Mark Zuckerberg rather dumbly stated, "Young people are just smarter," apparently forgetting that it was baby boomers like Tim Berners-Lee, Bill Gates, and Steven Jobs who led the information revolution and made his job (and all those hoodies) possible. Zuckerberg may be the poster child for entrepreneurship, but one obviously doesn't have to be a 20-something to be dreaming up something big. "The fastest growing demographic in the world of entrepreneurship is baby boomers," says Jane Robinson of MoxyMarketplace, finding plenty of evidence to back up that bold claim. Millions of boomers with two or three decades of corporate experience are taking their skills and passions to become "creative entrepreneurs"—people who build a business around their personal sense of aesthetics.[21]

Ewing Marion Kauffman Foundation, a not-for-profit organization that champions the concept of entrepreneurship, also found that there were more ventures launched by baby boomers over the past 10 years than any other age group. The share of new entrepreneurs aged 55-64 grew from 14 percent in 1996 to 23 percent in 2012, according to the foundation, a reflection of the two vital things many mid-lifers have in spades—time and money. A 2015 Gallup survey conformed that people over 50 were among the fastest-growing groups of new entrepreneurs in the United States (about twice that of millennials, in fact).[22] Weary of the corporate grind and not ready to sit on a beach, boomers are revisiting the creative passions they had as young people and packaging them as indie enterprises like art galleries or dance studios. The Internet has made much of this possible, of course, as reaching a global audience of consumers is today a lot easier than when boomers' parents were reaching what was then retirement age.

Some creative entrepreneurship among boomers is driven more by necessity. With no jobs or even interviews in sight (resumes listing college degrees granted in the 1970s are typically trashed immediately), boomers are creating their own businesses and never looking back at nine-to-five life. Ignored by dozens of potential employers because of his age,

64-year-old Jim Glay of Arlington Heights, Illinois, founded Crash Boom Bam, a vintage drum company, in his apartment's spare bedroom. While not making him rich, the unquestionably cool enterprise paid the bills, something the traditional job market certainly wasn't doing. Because of technology and the increasing irrelevance of geography, it's easier and cheaper than ever to start a business, making creative entrepreneurship a good option for boomers with a little imagination and a lot of determination. The desire to immerse oneself in a particular passion is often the backdrop for the decision to go off on one's own. After a 35-year career in information technology, 60-year-old Paul Giannone of Brooklyn decided to pursue his passion, which happened to be pizza. It required taking out a second mortgage on his home, but Giannone took the big leap of opening Paulie Gee's, which quickly proved popular among the borough's hipsters. "I wanted to do something that I could be proud of," Giannone said, feeling that being his own boss made his new job not feel like work.[23]

The stories surrounding boomers who changed their lives to follow their inner muse can sometimes seem like those of a Hollywood movie. The stress of working more than 80 hours a week in a law firm was making Antoinette Little sick, according to her doctor, forcing her to consider career alternatives. After taking a few culinary classes, Little discovered her passion: making chocolate. Voila! Antoinette Chocolatier in Phillipsburg, New Jersey, was born, offering her not just the chance to be a creative entrepreneur but to live a lot longer. "You get to eat your mistakes," she quipped, obviously a lot happier making truffles and other tasty treats than filing legal briefs.[24]

Given the huge number of potential creative entrepreneurs, it's not surprising that business start-up seminars specifically for boomers have become quite popular across the country. AARP, which calls someone over the age of 50 who starts a small business an "encore entrepreneur," is doing yeoman's duty by working with the Small Business Administration (SBA) to help boomers do just that. A webinar series and free online courses can be found at the SBA's Learning Center, and there are Encore Mentoring events in various cities as well. Attendees at these events get counseling and training to learn how to create their own enterprise, with the writing of a business plan and seeking of financing key steps along the way.[25]

Companies offering coaching and support for budding boomer entrepreneurs are another growing business, with Bizstarters leading the way. Since 1991, Bizstarters has helped boomers stay in the game after leaving a traditional job, often by doing something a lot more interesting and creative than in their first career. While age is a liability in the standard job market, it's a clear asset in the entrepreneurial world, according to Jeff Williams, founder of Bizstart. "People pay for expertise, experience, and wisdom, and baby boomers have it," Williams believes, with their network and project orientation other key plusses. Most of Bizstart's clients launch their venture in a few months for under $10,000, with Williams's team providing the bridge from idea to reality.[26]

OPPORTUNITY

Embed the spirit of creative entrepreneurism in your business to appeal to boomers.

VOLUNTEERISM

Another form of creative entrepreneurship is volunteering for an arts-based organization. Baby boomers are enlisting in droves to such organizations, so much so that some are calling the desire to contribute in some way to the arts the Volunteer Revolution. One-third of all boomers do some kind of volunteer work, according to a number of sources, making them nothing less than an army of more than 20 million people. The number of volunteers aged 65 and older is projected to climb nearly 23 percent to 13 million in 2020 from 10.6 million today, according to the Corporation for National and Community Service, a governmental agency focused on volunteering.[27] Again, boomers have significant amounts of that most valuable form of currency—time— and are willing to exchange some of it for self-satisfaction and the feeling of being valued. As well, boomers whose professional lives have ended find volunteering to be an excellent way to maintain a social network and stay connected with their community, each of these key to well-being in one's later years.

Alongside their countercultural schooling in creativity, boomers were immersed in the ethos of giving back to society in order to make the world a better place. The famous line included in JFK's Inaugural Address— "Ask not what your country can do for you, ask what you can do for your country," still seems to be ringing in many boomers' ears as they get involved in the nation's art scene *en masse*. As volunteers to museums and other cultural institutions, most of them nonprofits, boomers are bringing the same educational background and skill set they possessed during their professional careers. Today's volunteer is thus quite different from those of previous generations, with boomers seeking more involvement in everyday decision-making than typically afforded to nonpaid workers. Smarter leaders of arts-based organizations, many of them boomers themselves, recognize this and are using older volunteers in capacities that go beyond envelope stuffing, answering phones, or showing guests to their seats at performances.[28]

To that end, in many larger cities across the country, there are resources that matchmake experienced businesspeople with volunteer opportunities within arts organizations. For more than 40 years, in fact, the Arts and Business Council of New York (ABC/NY) has connected Gotham's business community with artsy organizations, a win-win initiative for all parties. The council's soup-to-nuts menu of services include serving on boards of directors and committees, designing websites, attracting larger audiences, planning for events, hiring and retaining the right people, and finding volunteers.[29]

Similar partnerships exist in other cities across the country. In Philadelphia, Business Volunteers for the Arts (BVA) helps manage creative not-for-profits and, in exchange, offers businesspeople the opportunity to engage with artistic people and enterprises. BVA's (unpaid) staff members contribute thinking in all key areas of business, including strategizing, finance, marketing, and people management. BVA annually supervises roughly 50 new assignments that range in length from three months to a year.[30] The Arts & Business Council of Chicago serves similar ends. Its force of more than 300 people consults to scores of creative and cultural organizations in addition to other arts-related nonprofits. Boomers comprise a large percentage of these volunteers, happy to lend their experience to a worthy cause and at the same time be a part of a creative institution. Those who volunteer their time do not have to join or contribute money to the organization with which they are working, but some are asked to join boards, particularly those with senior management experience (and, of course, those with deep pockets).[31]

Being a museum tour guide presents an alternative way for arts-loving boomers to volunteer. Speaking to groups about art offers a direct opportunity to be fully engaged in a creative realm, exactly what many boomers want to do if they are not artists themselves. More freewheeling docents have "gone rogue" by steering off script during tours, however, leading to some museums putting in place rather strict measures. The Metropolitan Museum of Art in New York requires a three-year commitment from its volunteer tour guides, while that city's Museum of Modern Art limits its volunteers to answering questions and providing information. New York's Whitney Museum of American Art, meanwhile, uses docents for public tours but has paid experts to guide student groups. In fact, becoming a volunteer at the Whitney is not unlike getting into an elite college. Just 30 or so docents are selected from more than a 100 candidates and about a third of those lucky ones drop out during the intensive training period, which requires at least a year of study of art history. Improving one's public speaking chops is also part of the Whitey's docent training, with lessons even given in gesturing and making eye contact. Those who don't make the grade are cut from the program, and those who do are dismissed if they fail to commit to at least one tour a week.[32] Talk about pressure!

OPPORTUNITY

Serve as a conduit for boomers to volunteer at arts organizations.

SUPERGIVING

Volunteering time is great, of course, but, as they say, it's money that talks. Throughout their lives, baby boomers have been generous givers to all kinds of causes, good news to nonprofits relying heavily on individual contributions. The even better news is that people tend to donate more money as they get older, subscribing to the truism that "you can't take it with you." Extended life spans mean boomers will be in their prime donor years longer than in previous generations, something that bodes well for the future of philanthropy. A recent study by the consulting company Age Wave in collaboration with Merrill Lynch Global Management found that boomers will donate over $6 trillion over the next 20 years, a windfall for institutions which align themselves with the groups' passions.[33]

Directly because of baby boomers' passion for all things creative, American museums are overall in good if not great financial health these days. Much of the fund-raising from the nation's top philanthropists is on the down low, but some museums have been cashing eight-, nine-, and ten-figure checks (yes, that would be $1 billion) from their richest patrons. The economic kerfuffle of 2008 triggered by the subprime mortgage fiasco is all but a distant memory to museum directors who are launching capital and endowment campaigns to raise very big money. Giving to arts, culture, and humanities nonprofits rose by around 22 percent to $16.6 billion between 2009 and 2013, according to a report by the Giving USA Foundation, much in part to a spike in American millionaires.[34]

Lots of small donations can add up quickly but, for museum directors, landing a "supergiver" is a more efficient means of raising the kind of money needed to take the institution to a new level. Such givers tend to be boomers, in part because younger people, except for some tech entrepreneurs, have yet to make their fortune. The Smithsonian Institution, the Norton Museum of Art of Palm Beach, Houston's Museum of Fine Arts, the Frick Collection in New York, Los Angeles County Museum of Art, the San Francisco Museum of Modern Art, and the Seattle Art Museum have all recently led capital campaigns focused on wealthy boomers, as that's where much of the money is. Fundraisers tend to go initially to an institution's trustees and inner circle, giving them first dibs on naming opportunities—the biggest prize in any philanthropic effort—with a fund-raising campaign directed to the public to follow.[35]

In 2013, for example, the Miami Art Museum changed its name to the Perez Art Museum Miami (PAMM) after Jorge M. Perez, an American billionaire real estate developer (and baby boomer) gave a gift of $40 million. Perez's story is a fascinating one and serves as a model of wealthy boomers' efforts to build a cultural legacy. After making his 10-figure number, Perez, like many of the American superrich going back to Carnegie and Rockefeller, shifted his focus from making money to how to best give it away. The passion of the immigrant son of Cuban exiles was art, making it natural for him to look first to the biggest museum in his adopted hometown of Miami as his beneficiary of choice. Expanding his scope from collecting art to enriching the resources of a public institution was also very much in the tradition of the greatest philanthropists of the past. Perez's hopes are to "make Miami a leading cultural capital and ensure his own legacy as a pillar of that change," a perfect blend of personal interests with civic ones. Perez's inner muse is not limited to PAMM; the man has also sponsored an artist residency program at the National Young Arts Foundation as well as Cuban and Argentine filmmakers at the Miami International Film Festival (and is producing films himself). "I have made more money than I ever thought anybody should ever make but that is not what I want to be remembered for," he recently said, preferring that his legacy be "for giving something back."[36]

As Perez's story makes clear, if there is a single reason to explain the explosion in giving to arts organizations, it is wealthy baby boomers' desire to leave a legacy. As Chapter 10, Footprints-in-the-Sand, will detail, boomers want to be remembered, and they are actively taking steps to achieve a kind of immortality, while they have the time (and money) to do so. Boomers following their inner muse are handpicking artsy organizations as their beneficiaries of choice, believing that having their name attached to such an institution will be just the thing to allow them to, in a sense, live forever. Others want to remain anonymous for various reasons but find comfort knowing they are helping to ensure the legacy of the institution they feel passionate about. The money can be used for a variety of things—a building extension, educational programs, acquisitions, or any number of other initiatives—with donors at that level able to specify how their millions will be put in play. Interestingly, donations to the arts and cultural organizations accounts for only about 5 percent of the total philanthropic pie, dwarfed by the two biggest areas, religion and education.[37] But boomers are as a group significantly less religious than their parents and significantly more interested in the arts, something that promises to shift the philanthropic mix over the next few decades.

OPPORTUNITY

Help all boomers regardless of their wealth to leave some kind of legacy.

FIVE

Bucket List

We live, we die, and the wheels on the bus go round and round.
Edward Cole (played by Jack Nicholson) in the
2007 movie *Bucket List*

You might have seen the movie. Two terminally ill guys of a certain age, billionaire Edward Cole (Nicholson) and mechanic Carter Chambers (Morgan Freeman) ditch their cancer ward and embark on an epic, round-the-world journey with an inventory of things to do prior to their demise. While the movie was so-so, the list was impressive:

1. Witness something truly majestic.
2. Help a complete stranger.
3. Laugh until I cry.
4. Drive a Shelby Mustang.
5. Kiss the most beautiful girl in the world.
6. Get a tattoo.
7. Skydive.
8. Visit Stonehenge.
9. Drive a motorcycle on the Great Wall of China.
10. Go on a safari.
11. Visit the Taj Mahal.

12. Sit on the Great Egyptian Pyramids.

13. Find the joy in your life.[1]

Happily, many boomers are writing bucket lists of their own and not waiting until they are terminally ill to scratch items off. A bucket list (as in "kicked the bucket") is an inventory of desired experiences in life that an individual did not get around to completing because he or she did not have the time, money, or initiative. By middle age, however, such a list looms large in the minds of many, as the recognition that one will run out of time at some point in the future becomes more real. Boomers are now heavily investing in bucket lists, sometimes literally so, with many more inventories of must-do-before-I-die experiences to be taken in the years ahead. The world is a very big place with an incredible array of things to see and do, but most of us live relatively narrow lives for most of our lives. A bucket list is a rare opportunity to step out of our little box and, as they say, better late than never.

Reaching a certain age, usually 60 or 65, is a common trigger to create a bucket list. Having some kind of health scare is another, and the death of a parent or friend could be yet one more reason to take stock of one's own life. Going to Europe or taking a cruise around the Caribbean might have been something boomers' parents did to fulfill a lifelong dream, but a 21st-century bucket list is far more diverse and active. Some experiences have become iconic or even clichéd—swim with the dolphins, ride a Harley down Route 66, or, as Cole and Chambers did, go on an African safari—while some are truly unique. Whatever the pursuit, marketers of all sorts have a golden opportunity to be part of this existential free-for-all.

OPPORTUNITY

Seize the day by offering boomers once-in-a-lifetime experiences.

ADVENTURE TRAVEL

Naturally, visiting places around the world that one somehow never got to during one's first or second acts is almost always included on bucket lists. European cities such as Paris, London, Rome, and Venice are staples on lists, although those are considered been-there-done-that for the already well traveled. Cruises are also popular, especially around the Hawaiian

Islands or through Alaska. The greatest hits of destinations on bucket lists are iconic sites such as the Great Wall of China, the Taj Mahal, Stonehenge, the Pyramids (all on Cole's and Chambers's list), Machu Picchu, Patagonia, the Amazon River, the temples of Angkor Wat, the Silk Road, the Serengeti (particularly during its great migration), the Himalayas, the temples and gardens of Kyoto, Easter Island, the Holy Land, and, now that it's opened up for tourism, Cuba.[2]

Some sort of geographic challenge is a common conceit of bucket lists, adding an extra cross-it-off-the-list dimension. Seeing all 50 states is a classic or, for something more difficult, visiting all 50 state capitals, as you might be surprised how small or remote some of those are. (Yes I'm talking about you Juneau, Alaska, and Carson City, Nevada). Real geographic nerds add stops to the five principal territories of the United States (Puerto Rico, the Virgin Islands, Guam, the Minor Outlying Islands, and my favorite, the Northern Mariana Islands) to their lists, or collect an A-Z list of countries.[3]

Some boomers are taking the RV trend of a few years back to new extremes. Retirees with wanderlust would sell their home and most of their belongings and hit the road, never quite knowing where their next stop would be. After staying in one place for many years, the point was to keep moving and enjoy the changing scenery and different kinds of people to meet across the country. Now, boomers are heading to different countries to live for a few years and then picking up stakes to move to another. Ever wondered what living in Finland would be like, or maybe Uruguay? Americans all-too-familiar with the rat race that defines much of life in these United States and who are ready, willing, and able to leave for undetermined periods of time are exploring the diversity of life in such places. The upsides are that the cost of living in many countries is cheaper than that of the United States and that the online universe has made where one happens to be in the world almost irrelevant; the downsides are the language barriers and that most nations place restrictions on how long visitors can stay. By that time, anyway, globetrotters are usually keen on rolling down the road to the next stop, wherever that may be.[4]

Bucket list traveling is often combined with engaging with some kind of wildlife. Visiting the Galapagos Islands understandably ranks high, as one will inevitably see loads of strange creatures while walking in the footsteps of Charles Darwin on the remote archipelago. Seeing penguins in the Falkland Islands (just off the southern tip of South America) became popular after the 2005 National Geographic film *March of the Penguins* was released. (Penguin trivia: there are five different species in the Falklands, none of them afraid of humans.) Spotting a wild panda in China is another much anticipated experience, as is getting within a little-too-close-for-comfort distance of polar and grizzly bears in Canada's northwest. For any American, there is literally not quite anything like blazing a trail through Borneo's jungles with a machete to see orangutans, tiptoeing through the Indian bush to get a glimpse of a Bengal tiger, or tracking a pod of whales from a RIB (Rigid Inflatable Boat) in Iceland. Hiking along Hawaii's Na Pali Coast to spy on birds found nowhere else on Earth or smelling the, well, pungent aroma of Tasmanian devils on that island off Australia are other rare pleasures to be had by more eco-oriented bucket listers. Although "Go on an African Safari" often makes lists, it's thankfully more about taking part in a game drive than taking home the head of a wild beast to put up on the wall of one's den. Kruger National Park in South Africa, Ngorongoro Crater in Tanzania, or Okavango Delta in Botswana are excellent places to see lions, rhinos, elephants, and other magnificent creatures in their local habitats.[5]

One might not think that the US Department of Agriculture was a business savvy organization, but its "Passport in Time" program is bucket list marketing at its best. Passport in Time (PIT) is a program offered by that department's forest service in which volunteers help preserve important archeological sites. Those who volunteer join real archaeologists and academics in various locations across the country to tackle tasks like doing excavations and surveys, restoring artistic rocks, researching archives, repairing historically significant structures, collecting oral histories, and analyzing and curating artifacts. A team of experts—historians, archaeologists, and conservationists—lead the projects. Since the formation of PIT in 1991, amateur archeologists have assisted in preserving thousands-of-years-old New Mexican cliff dwellings, unearthing an ancient Minnesotan settlement, rebuilding a notable Oregonian watchtower, scrubbing graffiti off Coloradan rock designs, plotting for potential digs in the rough Montanan backwoods, and uncovering an old Idahoan mine used by Chinese immigrants.[6] "Take Part in a Real Archeological Dig" may not be on everyone's bucket list, but it's just the kind of authentic travel experience many boomers want to have, at least once.

OPPORTUNITY

Take boomers to places they've never been but always wanted to go.

NOT-SO-CHEAP-THRILLS

Not surprisingly, given baby boomers' past penchant for altered states, experiences offering some kind of thrill are a staple on many bucket lists. As for Cole and Chambers, real-life boomers have an urge to jump out of an airplane, quite a rush and a means perhaps to confront fear head on. For many people, skydiving is one of those things that one wants to do just once, if only to know what it feels to plummet at a velocity of about 125 miles per hour with arms and feet fully extended (200 miles per hour if balled up). The duration of the ride depends on the elevation of the plane when one jumps. One freefalls for about 30 seconds from 9,000 feet, about sixty seconds from 13,000 feet, and about ninety seconds from 18,000 feet. The parachute will be deployed at around 5,000 feet, so one has another (more relaxed, presumably) four to five minutes before landing. FYI, you can't weigh more than 250 pounds to skydive, and no alcohol (or other drug) consumption is allowed before jumping. (That's for after.) Interestingly, a surprising number of people who are scared of heights take on the challenge of skydiving and later report that the experience was actually less frightening than, say, looking down from a tall building. Group skydiving with friends has become the thing to do among the more adventurous, with the whole thing videotaped to later show off to alarmed children wondering what the hell has gotten into their normally boring parents.[7]

Whitewater rafting is another not-so-cheap thrill that many boomers want to experience, especially through the Grand Canyon. There's no better Grand Canyon rafting outfitter than Grand Canyon Whitewater, which has been guiding folks down the Colorado River since the 1970s. Grand Canyon Whitewater rafting trips are giving bucket listers the opportunity to be in one of the most spectacular places on Earth and to truly get to know the Grand Canyon and the Colorado River. While rafting the river, one "shoots" rapids such as Crystal and Lava Falls when not slowly floating over smooth stretches of water. A typical day also usually includes a challenging hike or two up a side canyon, adding to the experience. One can sign up for motorized—or oar-powered rafting trips, some of them combining "hikes in" or "hikes out" of the Canyon. The 13-day oar trip allows rafters to take in the majesty of the entire Canyon, from the spectacular layers of rock in Marble Canyon and then through the Inner Gorge to Diamond Creek. After passing the Little Colorado River and Havasu Creek on the trip through Grand Canyon, one can investigate sites such as Redwall Cavern and Deer Creek Falls on extra hikes each day.[8] Needless to say, it's an unforgettable experience, especially if friends or family are along for the ride.

Other bucket listers are opting to scuba dive on the Great Barrier Reef in Queensland, Australia. That reef is the biggest and most robust network of coral in the world and the lone living organism on the planet that can be detected from above the Earth's atmosphere. The Great Barrier Reef is constructed of almost 2,900 separate reefs, 600 mainland islands, and 300 coral keys. Scuba and snorkel enthusiasts love the place for the incredible range of organisms to be seen (but not touched), and the native population considers it to be a hallowed element of their spiritual life, making it a truly magical place. Dives include Ribbon Reefs in the Northern Great Barrier Reef where, in the summer, one might see dwarf Minke whales and a plethora of other sea critters. Special boats take passengers to Osprey Reef from Cairns or Port Douglas, with the visible coral mesa smack dab in the Coral Sea distant from everything. North Horn is famous for its shark feeding, while Around the Bend flaunts rainbow-like soft coral and provides the possibility to spot manta rays moving through the reef. Sea turtles, potato cod, leopard moray eels, bumphead parrotfish, cuttlefish, sea snakes, and macro life are also teeming, making the reef literally like no place else on Earth.[9]

Much closer (and faster) to home is the NASCAR Racing Experience, which offers bucket listers the chance to drive real NASCAR racecars (passing allowed, in case you were wondering). With a car radio and a driver's meeting with a crew chief, it's as real as it gets, making it understandable why a gift certificate for the experience is a popular one among wives of boomers who've always wondered what it would be like to drive a car upward of 200 miles per hour. One doesn't even have to go too far to do it. The NASCAR Driving Experience can be had at 14 of the country's best tracks: Atlanta Motor Speedway, Auto Club Speedway in Fontana, California, Charlotte Motor Speedway, Chicagoland Speedway, Dover (Delaware) International Raceway, Homestead Miami Speedway, Kentucky Motor Speedway (in Sparta), Michigan International Speedway (in Brooklyn), Myrtle Beach Speedway, New Hampshire Motor Speedway (in Loudon), Phoenix International Raceway, Richmond International Raceway, Talladega (Alabama) Superspeedway, and Texas Motor Speedway in Fort Worth. For those who'd prefer to ride shotgun, there is the NASCAR Ride Along, with a racing pro taking passengers at very high speed for three white-knuckled laps.[10] Either way, bucket listers go home happy from their brush with racecar driving and are likely more content they chose a profession in which they sat behind a desk most of the time.

> **OPPORTUNITY**
>
> Package not-so-cheap-thrills into your brand's deliverables.

PASSION POINTS

Immersing oneself in personal passions, or what I call "passion points," understandably fills out many boomers' bucket lists. By midlife, any individual knows very well what he or she loves to do, making an item on a list an extreme version of a particular passion. The desire to have an as yet-to-be-fulfilled experience can be expressed in either quality or quantity. Foodies may want to eat in a certain restaurant somewhere in the world (Georges V in Paris comes up with unusual frequency), an example of taking one's gastronomic passion to the highest level possible. Quantity, that is, doing what one loves to do as much as possible, is the other way to go, the assumption being that more of something good will be better. Assigning a specific number of days within a year to enjoy one's passion is something more goal-oriented listers tend to do, with that number sometimes tied to one's age. A person 70 years old might declare that he or she will sail 70 days that year, for example, adding another day for every year.

You might be surprised how many astronomy geeks dream of observing a planet, star, constellation, or astronomical event they never have before. For them, "Seeing the Southern Cross" or "Count the Rings of Saturn" makes it onto their bucket list, usually by going somewhere where the artificial light from cities does not obscure the natural darkness. Cherry Springs State Park in Pennsylvania, one of the darkest spots east of the Mississippi, is one of those places. (The park is a Gold-Certified International Dark Sky Park, one of only a handful in the country.) For those putting "See a Meteor Shower" or "Witness a Lunar Eclipse" on their list, there is no better vantage point than Death Valley National Park in California. Professional astronomers rate the stargazing on top of Mauna Kea, the best on Earth, because of Hawaii's virtually zero light pollution, however, making that place a prime destination for the starry eyed. Denali National Park and Preserve is one of the best places to see the aurora borealis or northern lights, while the Atacama Desert in Chile is the spot to take in the rarely seen Tarantula Nebula and the Fornax Cluster of galaxies.[11]

For those who have a true passion for the sport, some sort of unusual golf experience is often near the top of a bucket list. Traveling to an exotic location with golf clubs in tow (Fedexing them is actually the way to go) can be just the thing to add some unforgettable moments to life's balance sheet, particularly if buddies share the same passion. The Verdura Golf and Spa Resort that overlooks the Mediterranean in Sicily is a good choice, for example, as is the Kauri Cliffs at Matauri Bay in New Zealand (with some of the course's holes played alongside the plunging cliffs above the Pacific). Duffers who also happen to be bird-watchers rank Falsterbo Golfklubb at the point of Sweden's Falsterbo Peninsula high, while others are lusting to play Elea Golf Club in Cyprus (which wends its way through olive groves) or Yas Links Abu Dhabi, which is situated on the Persian Gulf (and has more than a hundred sand traps!). Bolder boomers are keen on the Danang Golf Course (just an hour from Hanoi in Vietnam), Leopard Creek in South Africa (watch out for the occasional big cat), the Legends Golf & Country Resort in Malaysia (with courses designed by Jack Nicklaus and Arnold Palmer), and the Nirwana Bali Golf Club in Indonesia (where the hazards are made of terraced rice paddies).[12]

The biggest golfing bragging rights, however, go to those boomers who can say they played the single-hole course in Panmunjom, a town plopped in the middle of the DMZ between North and South Korea. That hole is legitimately labeled the "World's Most Dangerous Golf Course" given that a golf ball hit out of bounds might very well land in an active minefield (mulligans encouraged). In addition to playing courses that are decidedly off the beaten track, there are other bucket-worthy golf experiences. Combining Scotch tastings in Scotland or whiskey crawls in Ireland along with playing some of the best golf courses in the world is a dream come true for those who enjoy a wee (or not-so-wee) dram.[13] Also, some golfers who have yet to get a hole in one in their lives are determined to do so, sometimes including that feat on their list of must-dos by obsessively playing par-3 courses until a tee shot rolls into the cup.

Of course, all sorts of fantasy camps frequently populate boomers' bucket lists. Rock and Roll Fantasy Camp, for example, offers regular Joes the experience of living the life of a rock star, with real ones, for a few days. After counselors evaluate one's skill level and musical preferences, campers are given a list of songs to practice before their arrival. Rockers are then placed in a band of like-minded and equally skilled musicians, assigned a counselor as mentor, and get their own rehearsal studio. Daily master classes in instruments and vocals are followed by nightly jams. Guest stars pop into rehearsals, with autographs, photos, and questions welcome (e.g., "Did you really kill that chicken on stage?"). The climax of the experience is a live performance at a popular venue on stage in front of real rock 'n' roll fans (usually including friends and family). "Skills are gained, fears are conquered, friendships are formed, and music is created," says the Rock 'n' Roll Fantasy Camp, urging boomers to "Check this one off your bucket list!"[14]

OPPORTUNITY

Plug into boomers' passions when marketing to them.

CREATIVITY AND AESTHETICS

As Chapter 4 detailed, creativity and aesthetics make up a big part of baby boomers' DNA, making it expectable that many of them would want to express their inner muse via their bucket lists. Art workshops like those offered by Arts & Cultural Travel, an outfit catering to smaller groups, are just the kind of creative experiences likely to make it onto boomers' lists, especially those of women. Arts & Cultural Travel delivers much more than just staring at art in a museum; clients go "backstage" to artists' studios and participate in improvised tutorials from accomplished crafts-people. Workshops are an authentic, immersive experience, with partici-pants taken behind-the-scenes to learn how indigenous art is created and has been passed down through generations. Each workshop experience is "crafted to help you tap into your creative place while rediscovering the fine art of play," the company explains, whether it be studying photogra-phy in Belize, sketching and water coloring in Charleston, or weaving in New Mexico.[15]

"Write a Book" or "Finish My Book" is popping up on boomers' bucket lists, another reflection of the creative aspirations of the group. My being a writer, people who are convinced they have a great idea for a bestseller constantly approach me, with many would-be authors having a few scrib-bled pages tucked away at a drawer somewhere. Those boomers with more time on their hands are recommitting themselves to their literary pursuits, sometimes working with writing coaches to move forward with their respective projects. The kind of projects varies widely; some are fic-tion, with the beginnings of the Great American Novel perhaps residing in their desk. A roman à clef, or work of fiction whereby actual individuals or events pop up with disguised identities, is sometimes the genre of choice.

Others are nonfiction, with histories of a certain subject near and dear to the writer's heart sometimes the work in progress.

Writing a memoir or family history also regularly appears on boomers' bucket lists. Many a boomer is convinced that his or her life story (or that of a parent or grandparent who inevitably faced great obstacles to go on to achieve the American Dream) would make a great book, if it only could get written. Major publishers rarely pursue such stories, need it be said, but self-publishing through Lulu, iUniverse, or Amazon is now a perfectly respectable way to see one's name in print. Handing out copies to friends and family is a joyful experience, with perhaps a talk at the local bookstore icing on the cake.

For those whose favorite creative medium is cooking, "Become a Master Chef" is almost a given on a bucket list. Amateurs who can whip up quite the tasty meal for their family and friends know they're good but not in the same class as those who do it for a living. Reading *bon appetite* or watching *America's Test Kitchen* is fine, but there's nothing like cooking school to teach foodies how to play in the big leagues. There are many such schools around the world, but none shows up more on bucket lists than Le Cordon Bleu Paris. That school provides an array of relatively brief culinary adventures for people who love to cook. The courses take place in both regular and demonstration classrooms and offer students a real-as-it-gets professional chef experience. Each class is limited to 16 people, with a Le Cordon Bleu chef offering instruction in both technique and recipes. In "The Art of Cooking Like a Chef," for example, the culinary journey starts with a morning demonstration after which foodies get to sample the goods. Students then whip up a dish of their own with a chef showing the way. Bakers opt for the "Freshly Baked Pastries Workshop" where, alongside the river Seine, participants learn to master the art of making French croissants, chocolate rolls, and brioches. "You will be able to return home and dazzle your friends with your culinary wizardry!," Le Cordon Bleu promises, exactly what the bucket lister has in mind.[16]

Bucket list experiences steeped in creativity and aesthetics do not always require such mastery. Taking care of some unfinished business often serves as the basis for a bucket list item, something marketers can and should capitalize on. Had a final exam when The Who played the "Garden" in 1974 and did the whole *Quadrophenia* album? Busy getting married when the Rolling Stones came to town on their "Steel Wheels" tour in 1990? Now there's a chance for boomers just like you to exorcise those rock 'n' roll demons that have haunted for decades by seeing iconic bands and artists in one fell swoop. Desert Trip is a new music festival targeted to boomers who want (at least) one more opportunity to see their favorite artists or bands whose members are still very much alive and kicking. Held at the same venue as Coachella, the decidedly hipper music festival, in Indio, California, Desert Trip is a one-stop-shop to see performers like the Stones, The Who, Paul McCartney, Neil Young, or Bob Dylan. The clever promoters of Desert Trip are going right after bucket listers, in fact, positioning the three-day concert as a "once in a lifetime" event.[17] Concertgoers can finally say they saw the Stones perform "Satisfaction" or hear Paul McCartney sing a Beatles song, something of incredible value to those who consider such things as nearly religious experiences.

OPPORTUNITY

Cater to boomers' insatiable appetite for creativity and aesthetics.

GIVING BACK

Not everything on a bucket list has to involve a trip to one of the Great Wonders of the World, offer visceral thrills, or improve one's creative chops. In fact, the #2 item on Cole's and Chambers's fictional list was "Help a complete stranger," an idea that many boomers are embracing. As described more fully in Chapter 9, boomers are seeking out ways to give back to society, particularly by volunteering and mentoring. Including an other-directed item on one's bucket list is a sign that the boomer understands that a big part of completing life's journey usually involves doing what one can to improve the life of someone else, even if he or she has not yet met that person.

Some boomers in Los Angeles, especially empty nesters or those without kids, for example, are including "Join the Fulfillment Fund" on their bucket lists. The Fulfillment Fund empowers students through education, in the process transforming the lives of individuals and producing a positive domino effect throughout a whole community. Via formal education, mentoring, face-to-face advising from college counselors, and interactive, real-world experiences, the Fund shows students the opportunities of higher education, and changes their perception of what they can accomplish. The Fund's mission is to "make college a reality for students growing up in educationally and economically under-resourced communities," something that resonates with boomers who became the most educated generation in history. Bucket listers invest a little time by partnering with an individual student, not just by helping him or her with schoolwork but by going to activities like sporting events or concerts. Proving guidance and support is the primary job for a mentor, something many boomers are well prepared to do.[18]

Baby boomer bucket listing is part of the reason why "voluntourism" has emerged as a fast-growing segment of the travel industry. More than one-and-a-half million Americans are forking out $2 billion annually via voluntourism by helping out in orphanages, constructing schools, tutoring in English, or doing some other good work. Although young people (some no doubt interested in resume-building) make up most of the voluntourists, more boomers are contributing their time and energy to urgent initiatives around the world. Tutoring children in Honduras, assisting HIV/AIDS suffers in South Africa, or helping out after natural disasters like the 2010 earthquake in Haiti or the Japanese tsunami the following year are prime example of voluntourism. Animal lovers and environmentalists are nursing orphan elephants in Kenya or tending to birds affected by the 2010 Gulf of Mexico oil spill, these other examples of how boomers are enriching their bucket lists with some good karma.[19]

Happily, donating time and/or money to a particular charity or philanthropy often makes it onto many boomers' bucket lists. If there's a single organization to which boomers intend to contribute before they die, it may very well be Habitat for Humanity (HFH), a Christian-oriented nonprofit that "believes that every person should have a decent, safe and affordable place to live." HFH is present in almost 1,400 communities all over the United States and in more than 70 other nations, with Jimmy and Rosalynn Carter its most famous volunteers. HFH welcomes all people to work with them in partnership by building, renovating, and repairing houses virtually anywhere via volunteers and donated money.[20]

Contrary to popular belief, HFH does not give houses away. Rather, the organization's partner families buy the houses that they collectively build and renovate on a nonprofit basis. HFH homeowners put in many hours of their own time and energy (termed "sweat equity"), laboring right next to volunteers and neighbors. And versus just new construction, HFH operates in various other ways to make adequate, inexpensive housing a reality for many. Besides building new houses, the organization refurbishes standing structures across the country, especially in inner cities. HFH Home Preservation and Revitalization programs assist in the renovation of houses and entire neighborhoods, while its Disaster Response program is a grass-roots effort to tackle a host of challenges following a natural calamity. HFH's activism and collaborations are going a long way to bring attention to the important issue of global housing, more reason why boomers with a social conscious are signing up.[21]

While helping to build houses for those in need is certainly a noble pursuit, some boomers are deciding to match their personal passions with their own form of philanthropy. "Start My Own Charity" is appearing more frequently on bucket lists as boomers seek to customize and wield more control over their philanthropic efforts. The red tape involved with forming a nonprofit is considerable, but those who create one often report great satisfaction in knowing that their money and time is going to a cause in which they believe. A scholarship foundation, where money is given for educational expenses to students who meet specific criteria, is one avenue of giving that boomers are finding relevant and rewarding. Such boomers are combining bucket listing with the passion points outlined in Chapter 10, Footprints-in-the-Sand, a win-win scenario for all parties involved.

OPPORTUNITY

Enable boomers to give back by partnering with them
on worthy causes.

LESS IS MORE

Some boomers are taking a different track with their bucket lists by putting the philosophy of less-is-more into action. One's third act is the ideal time to streamline one's life, focus on family, explore different forms of spirituality, or find closure, with bucket lists an ideal vehicle to achieve any or all of those things. Rather than build a dream house, buy that '65 Corvette one always yearned for, or maybe outbid everyone at an auction to own a real Picasso (one of his drawings, at least), eschewing such materialism for the exact opposite could be the better path toward realizing a sense of closure. After acquiring things for decades, stuff-laden boomers are committing themselves to disposing everything in their houses that is not needed or has some genuine sentimental value. Giving things away or selling them is a liberating experience, many report, making them include "De-Clutter" or words to that effect on their lists. The added benefit is that one's children will not have to go through all the stuff when one dies or has to go to the Old Folk's Home—a real gift, as anyone who has gone through it can tell you.

Less is more can also be achieved through the simple act of knowing more about oneself. Genealogy-mania has made "Trace My Roots" a very popular item on boomers' bucket lists, with new tools available making that process a lot easier. Building a family tree and collecting stories about relatives of the past help place oneself in historical context, quite a powerful experience, as any watcher of Henry Louis Gate's *Finding Your Roots* show on PBS can tell you. Ancestry.com and 23andme.com each offer DNA testing for about $100 that reveals one's ethnic mix, the biological means to find one's roots. Exploring one's ancestry helps to "understand who you are, where you come from, and how you connect with the world," 23andme tells users, not at all an exaggeration.[22] Some boomers are going old school by going to their family's ancestral home, hoping to find relatives or other locals who could tell some stories about the past. There is nothing quite like sifting through century-old, dusty records in a village in Europe, it's safe to say, with the journey just as rewarding as the destination.

A related gift that boomers are bestowing through their bucket lists is the writing of letters to all their children and grandchildren. These letters (sometimes to be opened right away, other times upon the writer's death) tell each receiver what he or she has meant to the parent or grandparent, making them powerful missives of love (or sadly, something quite different). Not just words of advice but photos are frequently included in the letters, borrowing on the concept of "ethical wills." An ethical will (or "legacy letter") is a way to "share one's values, blessings, life's lessons, hopes and dreams for the future, and forgiveness with family," according to celebrationsoflife.net, making it one of the most meaningful and cherished things one could give to another person. A different spin on the same idea is a series of one-on-one meetings, allowing the bucket lister to personally express their feelings to each family member.[23] Including such an item on a list is an inspired and generous gesture, and one that more boomers are doing when they ponder what has mattered most in their lives.

Exploring different forms of spirituality is another core component of bucket lists. Regardless of one's faith, or even if one is agnostic, observing expressions of spirituality can be a deeply moving experience. Some boomers are making it a point to witness the call to prayer at the mosques at Isfahan in Iran, for example, and others to hear the Buddhist chants of monks in remote Tibet. Zegrahm Expeditions is hooking boomers up with such spiritual journeys, offering "adventures that few Westerners have ever experienced."[24] Other, more paganistic excursions tend to be a lot more fun. Perhaps hearing what a trip (sometimes literally) the Burning Man Festival in the Black Rock Desert is from their kids, quite a few boomers are finding themselves dancing naked through the night while a 40-foot wooden effigy is set afire, a classic bucket list experience.

Finally, finding a sense of closure is imperative for some baby boomers, making them include that often difficult challenge as an item (often the last) on their bucket lists. In many occasions, learning what happened to one's childhood best friend, college roommate, or first great love is the thing that boomers believe will provide this feeling of completion. For decades, perhaps, those "in the autumn of the year," as Sinatra put it, have laid awake in the wee hours of the morning wondering whatever came of a once important person in their life. Mending a relationship that ended badly is another common goal for closure-seekers. In the film *Broken Flowers* from 2005, Bill Murray's character goes on a cross-country search for a former lover and their alleged son, the kind of journey boomers wistfully imagine they could take to revisit their own personal past. With Google, Facebook, Classmates.com, and other online resources, finding a certain person is easier than ever, with often no need to even leave one's computer. Even contacting an old flame via social media takes some courage and commitment, however, as memories can reopen old wounds, as we all know. Still, many a boomer includes "Google the One That Got Away" on his or her bucket list, finally ready to face the truth, however painful or joyful that might turn out to be.

OPPORTUNITY

Align your brands with powerful, less-is-more experiences.

SIX

Higher Ground

This is the time in life to help you identify what has been stirring inside of you and what connects you to yourself at a soul level. It is the time to find your cause.

Diana Raab

Raab, who writes "The Empowerment Diary" blog for psychologytoday. com, might as well be speaking of this chapter, "Higher Ground."[1] Higher Ground describes the evolution of human beings in their third act of life, a concept with deep historical roots. "The key to growth is the introduction of higher dimensions of consciousness," wrote Lao Tzu, the ancient Chinese philosopher and father of Taoism, around 600 BC, not knowing that a couple of millennia later a generation known as baby boomers would take that idea and run with it. Higher Ground is about the big stuff of life—gaining experience and wisdom, realizing one's full potential, advancing one's spirituality, embracing aging, and, for some, passing it all on to grandchildren.

The ability to climb Higher Ground is in some respect a function of the peace of mind many boomers are beginning to experience as they head through their sixties and seventies. There is a common belief among boomers that one is now playing with house money, meaning they feel they have already lived a full life and anything good that happens to them at this point is a bonus. Every day is a gift to be appreciated and savored, they can say in all honesty, a wonderful luxury to be able to possess. The physical signs of aging are offset by an accumulation of personal growth and wisdom, I can personally attest, a function of life experience and a greater awareness of one's own mortality. Research does indeed show that aging does often bring a greater sense of well-being and emotional contentedness, with the demons of youth mostly gone and the compulsions of both id and ego mostly sated. Older people are slower to get angry and are more likely to see the bright side of complicated situations, studies also have revealed, with conflict-solving another skill acquired through experience. Also, boomers are prone to forgive and forget when things go south in a relationship, a reflection of their ability to see the bigger picture.[2]

How can marketers put the powerful idea of Higher Ground into action? Many ways, I believe. Contributing to boomers' feeling they are reaching Higher Ground is a good start, I contend, specifically by reinforcing the fact that the third act of life is the ideal time to experience a different level of joy and to realize one's full potential. More concrete expressions of Higher Ground are out there for marketers who think creatively. For example, Headspace, which wants to make the world a happier, healthier place through improved mind health, recently got together with the architect Oyler Wu Collaborative to locate "meditation pods" wherever large groups of people congregate. "We hope Headspacers will use them like Superman used phonebooths," says Rich Pierson, cofounder of the company, "only instead of emerging in tights intent on fighting crime, they'll come out with a clearer, calmer outlook."[3] Meditation pods are a great example of how boomers and everyone else can achieve Lao Tzu's "higher dimensions of consciousness" in everyday settings.

OPPORTUNITY

Elevate your brand as an agent of Higher Ground.

TRIUMPHS OF EXPERIENCE

Decades of research into life's rich pageant has led to some good news for baby boomers' third act of life: people continually progress as they get older and frequently realize greater fulfillment than when they were younger. Begun in 1938, the Grant Study of Adult Development charted the physical and emotional health of over 200 men, starting with their undergraduate days at Harvard University. (Harvard wasn't coed at the time.) The group of researchers tracked the students for the next few decades, measuring, testing, and interviewing them every few years to see how lives developed. The landmark book *Adaptation to Life* described the lives of the men until they reached the age of 55, offering key insights into how adults matured.[4]

As described in his follow-up book *Triumphs of Experience*, George Vaillant, who heads up the Study of Adult Development at Harvard University's Health Services Center, followed the men into their nineties, documenting what life was like for them in their later years. The findings? People who are content in their last third of life were not always so in their second, contradicting the widespread belief that older folks are as a rule sad and depressed whose best years are behind them. Being married leads to significantly greater satisfaction after turning 70, the study also reported, dispelling the myth that people who have been together for a long time eventually get tired of each other. The ability to move on from professional or personal disappointments was key to being happy, Vaillant found, with carrying regrets around for decades leading to a woulda-coulda-shoulda orientation to life. Savoring the things that had gone right was instrumental to later life, affirming the importance of seeing a partially filled glass as half-full rather than half-empty. Knowing that one had found meaning and purpose in life was understandably of great satisfaction, even if it took quite a while for that to happen. Interestingly, those who had had the capacity to establish intimate relationships with other people were not just more content but lived longer, proof positive of the importance of being engaged socially as we get older.[5]

In addition to spearheading the Grant Study, Vaillant has devoted a big part of his professional life investigating the relative contentment of boomers (partially to gain a better understanding of his father's depression). Vaillant has determined there are four typical characteristics of joyful boomers: empathy (identifying with others); engagement (remaining interested in life); hope (believing things will get better); and gratitude (thankfulness for what one has). Happily, so to speak, one can usually do something about how sanguine one is likely to be later in life, meaning we do not have to be victims of our genetic disposition. "We can keep changing and improving and become happier throughout life," he wrote in *Triumphs of Experience*, echoing the theme of Chapter 2, Old Dog, New Tricks.[6] Surrounding oneself with positive people is boomers' best strategy to be joyful in their third act, with love and support from others a far more effective antiaging technique than any pill or treatment. Boomers often report greater contentment after forming relationships offering amity or the chance to serve as a kind of counselor and even when devoting much of their own lives to the well-being of other people. Those boomers who've achieved the greatest happiness are those who have some mission in life (usually related to the welfare of others) and can access a network of trusted people to help out if personal problems arise.[7]

If there's any single most important implication from *Triumphs of Experience*, it's that boomers who are able to frame events in their lives in positive ways will be happier, more contented people in their third act. Those with flexible and positive personal narratives, that is, the stories they told themselves, will be more likely to "age well," with those feeling they took a wrong turn on their life journey more prone toward experiencing mental and physical health problems. What boomers think of their lives depends much on how well they have reconciled their major disappointments or failures, in other words, with a wide variety of strategies available for making peace with missed opportunities. The way to emotional well-being is to cultivate optimism and resiliency as life brings its challenges, with adapting to rather than resisting change a very good thing for boomers to do if they can.[8]

A new study suggests that most boomers are already experiencing triumphs of experience. Seventy-four percent of Canadian boomers are "in complete optimal mental health," research by a University of Toronto professor reveals, meaning they are happy almost every day. Versus millennials, baby boomers are more apt to be financially secure, share a relationship with a significant other, and be generally well grounded in life, all major contributors to one's happiness quotient. Interestingly, according to this 2016 study, the magic formula to well-being for both older and younger people is knowing someone with whom one can confide, with "complete optimal mental health" much more likely if there is a person around who is always "there for you," regardless of the circumstances.[9] Memo to readers seeking a sense of bliss in their third act: find a BFF (Best Friend Forever) if you don't already have one!

OPPORTUNITY

Celebrate boomers' triumphs of experience in your
brand communications.

PRACTICAL WISDOM

Baby boomers feeling they are making strides up their personal evolution ladder are often not just healthy and happy but wise, or at least in the general vicinity. For centuries, the extremely wise have tried to decipher what constitutes wisdom, but there is still no consensus on exactly what it is, how it's acquired, and how it can be best put to use. Despite differing views on the subject, wisdom is usually seen as the result of a collection of experiences that culminates in the most advanced stage of life that a person can reach. The continual development (intellectually, socially, emotionally, and morally) needed to attain this ultimate phase of life implies that wisdom keeps building throughout one's years. Wisdom is believed to result in more fulfillment, gratification, and a sense of well-being later in life and can be beneficial to others and society at large.[10] For all these very good reasons, many boomers are striving for wisdom, making it something that will heavily inform their third act of life.

Like that of previous generations, boomers' path toward becoming recognized as the wise elders of society is rooted in science. The association between wisdom and aging has a basis in biology: as humans get older, the mind further develops, a direct by-product of simply having living longer and experiencing more things. Older people are usually more proficient than young people in certain dimensions of cognition, particularly those that involve different ways to solve problems, as well as life planning and making future goals. Those deemed as "wise" are considered to have greater empathy, be more correct in their views of others' emotional status and be more thoughtful of the well-being of other people. Wisdom thus appears to incorporate a kind of "emotional intelligence" focused on relationships, accounting for why it is so revered. Should it be any surprise that older people serve as a font of wisdom for young folks, especially when it comes to relationships and making life decisions?[11]

The accumulation of wisdom appears to be nature's form of compensation for the body's insistence to age. Memory worsens as we get older, but research also seems to suggest that our strategy for the way that we process thoughts and information changes for the better. Older decision makers make significantly better choices by using their prefrontal cortex, where more rational, deliberative thinking is controlled. Scans of the brain reveal that younger adults typically employ just a single hemisphere to solve a particular problem, while older people will usually employ both parts of their noggins simultaneously—a process termed "bilateralization." Tapping into the full range of one's brain's power allows us to make more meaningful connections to a problem or situation. As individuals confront different situations, in other words, their brains form representations or cognitive outlines that enable them to detect and react appropriately when similar situations arise.[12] This natural and effortless flowing from the pool of experience that we have assembled through the years is, for lack of a better word, wisdom—a priceless asset that makes aging the rich, wonderful experience that it can be.

The value of wisdom as the tens of millions of boomers enter their third act is not going unnoticed by researchers. One institution—the University of Chicago's Center for Practical Wisdom—is leading the way in learning more about wisdom and seeing how it can be applied in real, everyday situations. Long ago, wisdom was considered a topic limited to arduous academic investigation in the noble pursuit of comprehending its makeup and value, making the center a throwback of sorts to the musings of the best and brightest of the ancients and Renaissance. It is indeed hard to conceive a topic that can better indicate what humans are capable of, with the center's leadership perceiving that a fuller exploration of wisdom promises to spark new ideas regarding how our species can flourish. The mission of the center is to "deepen the scientific understanding of wisdom and its role in the decisions and choices that affect everyday life," an admittedly ambitious undertaking. "We want to understand how an individual develops wisdom and the circumstances and situations in which people are most likely to make wise decisions," these modern-day Socrates declare, "hoping that, by deepening our scientific understanding of wisdom, we will also begin to understand how to gain, reinforce, and apply wisdom and, in turn, become wiser as a society." Specific questions the center's researchers are asking are "What is the relationship between expertise and wisdom?," "How does experience increase wisdom?," and "What is the relationship between cognitive, social and emotional processes in mediating wisdom?"[13]

Rather than simply ponder such big questions of life, the Center for Practical Wisdom is putting its money where its mouth is. The center is connecting scientists, scholars, educators, and students at the University of Chicago with researchers and scholars internationally who are interested in studying and understanding wisdom and is leading the way in knowing more about the dynamics of wisdom, commissioning fresh research in the area, and publishing what was discovered. The center is also working to increase public interest in wisdom, in increasing personal wisdom, and in the notion that even our institutions could become wiser.[14] Wise words indeed!

OPPORTUNITY

Offer boomers ways of wisdom as its cultural currency increases.

SELF-ACTUALIZATION

You remember the chart from a college psychology class. In his pyramid-shaped Hierarchy of Needs, Abraham Maslow proposed that there are five stages of life that people confront as they age. People are motivated to achieve certain needs, he wrote way back in 1943, the most basic one being physical survival. One has to satisfy a lower need before progressing to a higher need, with our orientation to life and much of our behavior dedicated to climbing the next step.[15] The original hierarchy (he later expanded it) is:

1. Biological and physiological needs: air, food, drink, shelter, warmth, sex, sleep
2. Safety needs: protection from elements, security, order, law, stability, freedom from fear
3. Love and belongingness needs: friendship, intimacy, trust and acceptance, receiving and giving affection and love, affiliating, being part of a group
4. Esteem needs: achievement, mastery, independence, status, dominance, prestige, self-respect, respect from others
5. Self-actualization needs: realizing personal potential, self-fulfillment, seeking individual growth and peak experiences[16]

While Maslow argued that just one out of a hundred people make it to the fifth, ultimate stage, not a single baby boomer had yet been born when he first conceived his hierarchy. The affluent society of the past half-century has enabled many boomers to march up the pyramid toward self-actualization—a remarkable thing if one believes the motivational theory of psychology has merit in real life. The self-help movement and development of a heavily therapeutic culture have also helped to push boomers up the pyramid; these are other major social forces that Maslow or anyone else could not have predicted when he published his landmark paper during World War II. Today, self-actualization has emerged as a common goal among more psychologically secure boomers, and it is something that will become even more prevalent as they move through their final act of life.[17]

Although people are more likely to use terms like "well-being" and "betterment" rather than "self-actualization," the idea is basically the same. As trendwatching.com recently noted, boomers are actively trying to achieve the idealized version of themselves as part of their endless quest for self-improvement. Fighting the physical signs of aging is no doubt (and unfortunately) accounting for a large chunk of boomers' discretionary dollars, but at least as much is being spent by them to become more of their authentic selves. In fact, much of contemporary consumerism is really about self-actualization, with brand choices made based on their relative ability to enable people to climb Maslow's ladder. "Consumers have moved beyond products as status symbols, and even moved beyond the 'experience' economy, to a place where self-actualization is the new status symbol," the smart folks at Trendwatching suggest.[18]

In fact, not just health or wellness is a path leading toward self-actualization but well-being in all dimensions of life, an idea that presents major opportunities for marketers of all kinds. Fostering a holistic, 360-degree sense of well-being and helping to provide a deep, emotional relationship between people and things and experiences are now how companies should define their vision and mission. "Self-actualization is the new carrot everyone is chasing," Melissa Thompson wrote in newsblaze.com in 2016, thinking that "the potential for people to self-actualize is higher than it has ever been before."[19]

Little did Maslow know that three-quarters of a century after his "A Theory of Motivation" article appeared in the academic journal *Psychological Review*, self-actualization would become a central theme of American society. The later years of life of what was the biggest generation in history are for many a time not to reflect on past achievements but to continue to realize one's full potential. For the man who coined the term, self-actualization was the desire for fulfillment or, in his own words, "to become everything that one is capable of becoming." Work has a lot to do with self-actualization, of course, with much of fulfillment to come from doing what we love and (and believing it is worth doing). It is at this intersection that we will find meaning, Barbara Sher explained in her book *I Could Do Anything If I Only Knew What It Was*, adding that we are lucky to live in a time and place when and where a good number of us have the ability to choose our careers.[20] Such a viewpoint is all the more reason why blatant ageism in the workplace is such a bad thing. Boomers who are immediately disqualified for jobs because of their age are effectively being blocked from their natural course of self-actualization, not just an illegal act but an unjust one. The Founding Fathers didn't mention it in the Constitution, but one of Americans' inalienable rights is the ability to try to become self-actualized, something many boomers are determined to do.

OPPORTUNITY

Define your brand as an opportunity for boomers to realize
self-actualization.

THE SPIRITUAL MARKETPLACE

For some boomers, reaching higher ground means becoming more spiritual, something that is completely consistent with the historical pattern of individuals finding religion in their later years. Whether greater spirituality is part of the process of becoming a more evolved human being or more about a greater awareness of one's own mortality, boomers are pondering deep thoughts about the meaning of life and what might come next.[21] For a good number of boomers, finding a little or a lot more faith is a kind of coming full circle. America was a much more religious place in the 1950s and 1960s, and kids were likely to get a heavy dose of traditional Judeo-Christian dogma.

Organized religion was perceived as part of the "system" many boomers found to be overly authoritarian as they became young adults, however, making them look elsewhere to fill spiritual needs. And as Wade Clark Roof showed in *Spiritual Marketplace: Baby Boomers and the Remaking of American Religion*, religion in this country fragmented over the past half century to the point where individuals could choose from a very large menu of alternative forms of faith. As Chapter 1 showed, Eastern philosophies especially informed boomers approach to spirituality, as did the New Age movement. (Remember the angels craze and *The Celestine Prophecy* sensation of the early 1990s?) "The quest culture created by the baby boomers has generated a 'marketplace' of new spiritual beliefs and practices and of revisited traditions," Roof wrote, with "some Americans exploring faiths and spiritual disciplines for the first time, others rediscovering their lost traditions, others drawn to small groups and alternative communities, and still others creating their own mix of values and metaphysical beliefs."[22] Around 85 percent of Americans believe in some kind of God, the Baylor Longitudinal Study of Religion showed, but only about 30 percent attend a church, synagogue, temple, or mosque, hard evidence of this cultural shift from religion to spirtualty.[23]

Boomers' gravitation to a myriad of personally defined avenues of spirituality reflects their gradual realization that they are part of something much, much bigger than themselves. Boomers are likely to construct their individual concept of spirituality based on their internalized belief system, overarching view of the world, and perceived role in life itself. For those open to such things, achieving greater harmony with one's inner self is a big part of the process, as is the desire to identify a larger sense of meaning and purpose as they age. And versus the greatest generation, baby boomers are more apt to speak in terms of spirituality versus religion, the gerontologist Vern Bengston has noted, opening up a broader range of theological avenues.[24]

Despite this and all other evidence to the contrary, Bengston and other experts are predicting that boomers will return to traditional religion as they get older much like how previous generations did, thinking that this is a basic part of the aging process. Based on the results of a recent Gallup poll, Frank Newport (editor-in-chief of Gallup) predicts that religion will have a more prominent place in American society over the next 20 years. Newport makes the case in his book, *God Is Alive and Well: The Future of Religion in America*, arguing that the baby boom generation will evolve into an increasingly religious demographic. Newport wasn't sure whether boomers would return to the faith of their upbringing or discover new forms of spirituality but felt confident they would find religion in their later years.[25] While some boomers may go back to traditional Christianity or Judaism, more are likely to continue to forge their own spiritual paths in the years and decades ahead.

Meanwhile, leaders of religious institutions are actively looking for ways to recruit more boomers into their flock. One more popular way is to integrate elements of Buddhism into Christianity or Judaism, thinking that such a fusion of Eastern and Western spiritualities is a best-of-both-worlds approach. Jews in particular are blending dimensions of Buddhist philosophy with their faith, hence the growing number of "JuBus." (A "JuBu" refers to "someone with a Jewish background who practices some form of Buddhism," according to Ellen Frankel of the *Huffington Post*.) Although a good number of Jewish people relate to many dimensions of their religion, many say the spirituality component is less than fulfilling.[26]

Those of a traditional Jewish background looking for a more powerful brand of spirituality frequently locate it in Buddhism, specifically its meditative and mindful techniques. As well, Buddhist philosophy does not focus on God, so Jews (and those of other faiths) are able to subscribe to it without having to give up their theism. Other reasons for those of a Jewish persuasion to be drawn to Buddhism is one, there is no history of conflict between the two groups; two, it isn't necessary to officially adopt

Buddhism as one's principal faith to practice it; and three, both Jewish and Buddhist people have a long history of sorrow. "As Jews continue to explore Buddhism and its practices, more JuBus will be able to discover the 'OM in ShalOM,' creating a rich and fruitful spiritual path," Frankel wrote, a nice way of describing how boomers of all faiths will shop at the bountiful spiritual marketplace in the future.[27]

OPPORTUNITY

Capitalize on boomers' interest in all kinds of expressions of spirituality as they age.

CONSCIOUS AGING

You may not have noticed, but a backlash against the negative ways in which aging is perceived in America is in the works. More and more boomers are embracing the idea of "conscious aging," in the process reaching higher ground in their own lives. Rather than deny the reality that people get older, conscious aging not only acknowledges that fact but celebrates it, turning the whole idea on its head. Conscious aging is thus not just a positive thing for individuals to do but a means of creating a healthier, less ageist society.[28] By "aging consciously, we will naturally begin to manifest those qualities that our society needs in order to survive," the spiritual guide Ram Dass wrote in his *Still Here: Embracing Aging, Changing, and Dying* (a reference to his earlier classic *Be Here Now*), those qualities being "sustainability, justice, patience and reflection."[29]

The Conscious Aging Alliance (CAA), a network of a dozen organizations committed to an empowering vision of later life, offers the definitive explanation of the concept:

Conscious aging is a perspective that sees aging as a life stage full of potential for purpose, growth, and service to community, and as a path toward realizing that potential. Our beliefs, about what is possible for us, and the intentions that spring from them, hold great power in shaping who we become. A great many baby boomers, as well as those further along in years, are hearing an inner call to age consciously, and are seeking support in responding to that call.[30]

As the CAA correctly explains it, conscious aging is steeped in the truism that over the course of thousands of years, many civilizations venerated those who had lived the longest, a practice that was viewed as important to the health of the whole society. Older people were termed "elders"—individuals assigned the key task of serving as mentors to younger people. Elders also were responsible for reciting the narratives that related the story and central beliefs of the society in order to ensure the well-being of future generations. Elders were seen as having evolved into a position of individual completeness so that they could act as role models for their community. Despite widespread ageism, the CAA continues, there is nonetheless a primal human drive to permit the "inner elder" to surface. Encouraging this to happen is the essential mission of conscious aging. "This is the work that can lead to wholeness and fulfillment as we age, in whatever circumstances life presents us," the CAA concludes, a worthwhile effort.[31]

Another organization actively promoting the cause of conscious aging is the Institute of Noetic Sciences (INS). Established by astronaut Edgar Mitchell (after having what he described as a "peak experience" while in space on the Apollo 14 mission), the INS is a "nonprofit organization dedicated to supporting individual and collective transformation through consciousness research, transformative learning, and engaging a global community in the realization of our human potential." (*Noetic* is Greek for "inner or intuitive knowing.") The goal of the INS is nothing less than to "create a shift in consciousness worldwide—where people recognize that we are all part of an interconnected whole and are inspired to take action to help humanity and the planet thrive." Part of the INS's charter is to train facilitators to lead Conscious Aging Workshops as a means of fostering spiritual, emotional, and psychological growth among those in their third phase of life.[32] To that point, the INS has recognized nine actions to help older individuals fully embrace being alive in our society where, unfortunately, many wish boomers would just go away:

1. "Reflect on your worldview, beliefs, stereotypes, and assumptions, and ask how might they be limiting you or holding you back;
2. Reframe your inner talk by making internal, critical messages more positive and self-compassionate;
3. Shift your perspective away from the popular media that shape the dominant view of aging and find opportunities to find joy and goodness;
4. Practice mindful attention by bringing your attention toward greater self-awareness;
5. Set intentions by asking yourself, 'What matters most? and 'What values do I want to adhere to?';

6. Build new habits by challenging your brain with new learnings, exploring new activities, or doing something new every day;

7. Find guidance by connecting with others offering a way of living into new patterns and behaviors;

8. Move from I to We in order to add joy and purpose to your actions;

9. Recognize that death makes life possible."[33]

OPPORTUNITY

Champion the worthy cause of conscious aging when
targeting boomers.

THE GRANDPARENT ECONOMY

Talkin' 'bout my generation? Not likely if there's grandkids around. Baby boomers are consumed by their grandkids, carrying on a long tradition of grandparents spoiling their children's children. As would be expected with an aging population, the number of American grandparents is high and still growing. There were about 65 million grandparents in the country in 2010, a study by the MetLife Mature Market Institute reported, a number that represented an-all-time-high. Because the number of grandparents is growing at twice the overall population rate, however, there will be even more of them. In 2020, the number of grandparents is projected to be 80 million, or nearly one of three American adults, according to the MetLife report.[34] And rather than little old ladies and men puttering around the house and knitting sweaters, most grandparents are active-as-ever boomers, casting a much different light on what older people look and act like. As with the attempt to come up with a better alternative to "seniors" or "elderly," in fact, some are trying to replace the term "grandparent" with a new one that does not automatically conjure the image of *Whistler's Mother*.

However they're referred to, boomer grandparents (grandboomers?) are spending big bucks on their grandkids and are more than happy to do so. For the generation that views virtually every aspect of life as an opportunity to grow, improve, and express themselves, grandchildren represent a prime way to achieve higher ground. Just like being a parent, being a grandparent means taking on a different identity, specifically by assuming a new set of responsibilities grounded in caregiving, nurturance, and love. Boomers' interest in their grandkids goes well beyond bouncing a grandkid on one's knee or taking him or her out for the occasional ice-cream cone. Many 60-somethings who are still working are not just putting money away for themselves but for their grandchildren as well, often through a college savings account.[35]

In addition to investing in grandkids' future educational costs, boomer grandparents are springing for a car when their grandchild reaches driving age or picking up the tab for a Sweet 16 party or family vacations. There's also considerable spending on less glamorous but quite expensive items like car insurance, rent, clothes, and school supplies—things parents often expect their kids to pay for themselves. "Boomer grandparents are taking grandparenting to the next level and not standing back waiting to be invited into their grandchildrens' lives," explained Lori Bitter, publisher of *Grand*, an online resource for grandparents and author of *The Grandparent Economy: How Baby Boomers Are Bridging the Generation Gap*.[36]

The best news about the grandparent economy is that boomers are not just spending money on grandkids but also time, seeing that as an investment that will pay off big dividends down the road. As always, grandparents are filling in for parents because of the latter's work schedules or when mom and dad want to have a date night. Bitter has observed more grandparents with grandchildren than parents with children at toy stores, prime evidence of the grandparent economy. With both time and money, boomers are throwing themselves headlong into the grandparent experience, some of them, for better or worse, even defining it as the centerpiece of their lives.[37]

Although mostly getting an A for effort, the eternally youthful generation becoming the largest generation of grandparents is admittedly a strange notion. Get-in-touch-with-your-feelings boomers reinvented parenting, many would agree, so are they now reinventing grandparenting? The majority of boomers were in full career mode while raising their kids, with finding the right balance between work and life a difficult challenge. This time around it's different, with boomers having a lot more time to spend with their children's children. (As well, diaper, car seat, and stroller technology have advanced immeasurably over the past 30 years and, needless to say, Skype and FaceTime were not around.)[38] Being in a supportive versus lead role is not easy for many boomer grandparents, however, particularly for a generation raised to speak their minds and to not sit on the sidelines of life. "Becoming a grandparent for the first time is like revisiting an exotic country that you loved long ago, only to find that everything's changed," observed K.C. Summers of AARP Media, finding "the experience is just as wonderful as ever but it takes a while to get your bearings."[39]

To help get her bearings, Summers, like many first-time boomer nanas, signed up for a grandparent class, which are increasingly being offered at hospitals and senior centers. It is not surprising that the generation who approach everything as a field to master are taking classes to learn how to be the best grandparent they can possibly be. "The boomer generation is cresting, their kids are having kids, and they want to be involved," said Ellen Breslau, editor-in-chief of grandparents.com, thinking that "the kids keep the grandparents young and the grandparents can share their wisdom and learning."[40] More engaged than their own grandparents were, boomers are finding themselves in a symbiotic relationship with their grandkids, often a win-win situation for all.

OPPORTUNITY

Invest in the grandparent economy as more boomers join its ranks.

SEVEN

Boomerpods

It takes a village.

Baby boomer Hillary Clinton (borrowing an
African proverb)

Who put the commune in community? Baby boomers. Thinking their parents' generation was becoming increasingly isolated in the 'burbs, many boomers in their first act of life assumed more of a group identity, sometimes even moving in with each other to form large, egalitarian households. The utopian dream of self-sustaining, leaderless communities didn't last long (even hippies didn't like to wash dishes, apparently), but the sense that one should belong to something bigger than oneself lasted well past the far out days of the counterculture. Community remains an essential strand in boomers' DNA, an attribute that will serve them well in their later years.

Boomers' natural leaning to create communities is in part a function of their being what was the biggest community in history. While youth culture in the 1920s certainly got people's attention, boomers became recognized as a distinct generation or "cohort" as soon as they were born after World War II. Boomers (and marketers) learned quickly there is power in numbers, something that still holds true today despite the media's fascination with millennials. With many boomers now empty nesters, their desire to get together with people who share something in common is arguably stronger than ever. Many such communities are somehow rooted in the past; there is a deep yearning to reconnect with people who were once important in their lives.

Boomers are not just looking back but forward, however, especially when it comes to forming meaningful relationships. This chapter, Boomerpods, proposes that boomers are in the process of forming new kinds of connections, friendships, and alliances, strengthening the role of community in their lives. A "boomerpod" is a close-knit community shared by boomers and characterized by strong personal or professional affiliations. The concept of boomerpods (my term) is backed up by studies indicating that belonging to a social network is good for older people's minds and bodies. It is vital to be around other people, in other words, especially later in life. Boomerpods will become more important in the years ahead as American society further fragments, I believe, with groups of people having something in common banding together in an increasingly diverse country (and world).

For marketers of all kinds, the concept of boomerpods is obviously an important one. It is easy to see how communities of passion represent an ideal way to reach boomers and fertile territories in which to seed brands. The beauty of community is the synergy that results when people get together; whatever comes out of the collective group is almost always "greater than the sum of its parts," as Aristotle put it. There is thus a significant opportunity for companies to plug into existing and emerging boomerpods in order to build strong alliances with boomers, with all sorts of communities— alumni networks, professional organizations, sports teams, and even band fans—good examples of such pods.

OPPORTUNITY

Think of boomers in terms of communities rather than as individuals.

AARP

Like many baby boomers, I shunned joining AARP, the nonprofit, non-politically partisan organization helping 50+ers make their lives better in some way, when it first approached me when I reached the half-century mark. I didn't want to be part of any group made up of old people, I thought at the time, in full denial that I was entering the third act of my life. Pretty soon after that, however, I later eagerly signed up when I learned of the great discounts to be had, making me, like 38 million others, part of this boomerpod of boomerpods. AARP is much more than getting 10 percent off your hotel room, however; the organization is the loudest champion of antiageism, a movement that will no doubt grow over the next couple of decades.

As I showed in my *Aging in America*, the founding of AARP (until 1999 the American Association of Retired People) in 1958 was an important milestone in the history of aging in America and a result of the emergence of what was then considered a new life stage. "Retirement" was a reaction to what was commonly seen as the major social problem of older people in mid-century America, transforming what A. Barry Rand, CEO of the organization between 2009 and 2014, described as a "life in purgatory" to a much desired destination. Since she became the CEO of AARP in 2014, Jo Ann Jenkins has been on a self-described "mission to disrupt aging," meaning she intends to "change the conversation around what it means to get older." Rather than pretend aging doesn't exist or take the position that being 50 is like being 40 or even 30, Jenkins believes people should embrace whatever age they actually are. Taking pride in one's age is an act of self-empowerment, she understands, and not unlike the process other marginalized groups have experienced in order to gain greater self-respect and social power. As with race, gender, or class, being defined by one's age is a silly and ignorant practice, and something that has to change if older Americans are to realize their deserved equal rights in everyday life.[1]

Charlotte Yeh has echoed Jenkins's spot-on philosophy of aging in the United States, further establishing AARP as a vital community for boomers. Yeh, chief medical officer at the organization, notes how "stubborn" the myths surrounding aging are despite all the research showing that the later stage of life is ripe for well-being. It is the persistency of these myths and stereotypes that diminishes the possibilities among Americans aged 50 or older, she maintains, serving as a device that places restraints on older people along many dimensions. It is steadily downhill after reaching the "prime of life," the basic story goes, that long slide bringing on a con-tinuous shrinking of physical, mental, social, and romantic powers. And because aging is seen as something that unfortunately "happened" to us, Yeh continues, it forces the oldest members of society into a victim-like role, a mind-set that demands rethinking as boomers rush headlong into their senior years.[2]

To its credit, AARP is taking ageism head-on and showing how the third act of life can be one's best. As its tagline "Real Possibilities," suggests, the organization delivers on its mission to help people turn their goals and dreams into realities, strengthen communities, and fight for the issues that matter most to families. On its website, AARP provides an abundance of useful information, including sound advice on health, money, relationships, style, work, and retirement. The organization also helps visitors to its site wade through the Byzantine universe of Social Security and Medicare and offers valuable resources for those facing the challenges of caregiving for loved ones. Career-related resources include job hunting tips, a search tool, advice on starting a business, and musings on the workplace difficulties that anyone 50 or older is likely to face. AARP's "Life Reimagined" initiative is particularly beneficial. "Life Reimagined is a vision, a methodology, and a community that helps people rediscover what truly matters and focus on what they really want to do," the organization explains, with leading experts in the fields of well-being, relationships, and work providing thought leadership and programs to "help you become more of who you truly are."[3] Additional information on volunteering and joining the fight for social change regarding ageism is icing on the cake.

Most card-carrying AARPers, however, are probably most interested in the discounts and benefits that members can enjoy. Deals can be had in a plethora of AARP-approved products and services covering retail, automotive, travel, entertainment and dining, financial services, health care, and insurance, making membership well worth the $16 annual fee. In addition to "Hot Deals," its Everyday Savings Center includes 25 electronics brands, 160 apparel brands, 89 home brands, 28 ticket brands, 40 gift brands, 10 auto brands, and 19 computer brands. "Whether you use your benefits to book your dream vacation or to save money on everyday purchases, your AARP membership can help you be your happiest, healthiest self," the organization tells those thinking of joining up, a compelling carrot to dangle before anyone looking to save money.[4] AARP is a guiding force of aging in America and the undisputed heavyweight champion of boomerpods.

OPPORTUNITY

Make AARP partnerships a staple of your marketing
efforts to boomers.

HOUSESHARING

Chapter 3, Reboot, showed how many boomers are foregoing the Del Boca Vista of *Seinfeld* fame for alternative housing situations. The massive condominium complexes in Florida and other warm spots were the cat's meow for the greatest generation when they got older, but their children are finding them to be too generic and institutional for their tastes. "Baby Boomers are throwing a wrench into the retirement housing market, rejecting the senior ghettos represented by cookie-cutter retirement communities and condominiums of days past, for new forms of affinity living and aging-in-place strategies," Laurel Kennedy of Chicago-area consultants Age Lessons wrote, with many different permutations of households springing up.[5] The explosion of multigenerational and blended families living together is part of this new model of boomer-based housing, as is the need to stay close to where one works. As well, most boomers want to be part of a heterogeneous community with an active social scene, even if not the kind of Hipsterville described in Reboot.

Although lifestyle-based communities like Worldmark Bison Ranch in Overgaard, Arizona (where residents mosey around as 21st-century cow-people), Rainbow Vision in Santa Fe (one of about two dozen villages for older GBLTs), and Sunset Hall in Los Angeles (comprised of "free thinking elders who continue to share independence of spirit and involvement in the world") are certainly interesting, the most significant development related to boomer housing is the group living arrangement. Life is imitating art in the unlikely setting of *The Golden Girls*, the 1980s sitcom in which a group of women of a certain age take up digs with each other. "Boomers are forming their own mini-communities based on longstanding friendships and shared interests," Kennedy observed, with both women and men "pooling funds, purchasing homes, and creating an extended faux family unit."[6] Part countercultural commune, part college dorm or sorority/fraternity house, housesharing is grounded in boomers' lifelong commitment to kinship, and an idea that is well suited to the one out of every three singles who do not want to live alone.

Women in their fifties and sixties in particular are exploring the possibility of buying a house or apartment building with a few friends with the intent to live together. The ability to take care of each other when needed is a compelling reason to go down the housesharing path, as is the desire to avoid social isolation. Another reason is of course financial; sharing costs with housemates makes a lot of sense, especially for divorced women or widows who do not have a large income. Such women sometimes find themselves with a large house that they are unable to maintain, making a search for those in a similar boat a sensible solution. Moving into a grown child's home is an option for the unattached, but that situation often makes the parent feel like a dependent, not a positive thing. Housesharers actually tend to be independent people who live their own separate lives but come together in different combinations for meals or chitchat. Folks find each other through networking or through a post on Craigslist or another classified advertising website (sometimes with the headline "GOLDEN GIRLS HOUSE").[7] There's even a nationwide Golden Girls Network where one can find the right roommate to share one's home. "Our network is a group of single mature women and men who love the idea of shared living with others and who are looking for an economical lifestyle by forming senior communities together," say the people at goldengirlsnetwork.com, a good example of the kind of boomerpods that are emerging.[8]

Best of all, "boomer roomies," as they are sometimes called, are finding peace of mind by living together. The oil and water relationship of *The Odd Couple* notwithstanding, straight people of the same gender can share an apartment or house without driving each other crazy. For those with health issues, housesharing is proving to take off some of the heavy burden of caregiving, as roomies assume a share of the responsibilities that friends, family members, and visiting nurses carried. A related living arrangement that is also getting more popular is the "pocket neighborhood," in which people choose to live in the same area and watch out for each other. Neighbors often cook and do errands with and for each other, a traditional way of communal living that hearkens back to a much earlier time. In fact, some experts believe an "aging in community" movement is afoot, equivalent to the home-based "aging in place" movement that is already sweeping across the country.[9]

Rather than wait for pocket neighborhoods or "cohousing communities" to take shape organically, visionary architects like Charles Durrett are building them. "Cohousing, by design, is a social agreement where people know about you, care about you and support you," says Durrett, who helped to import the model to the United States from Denmark in the 1980s. Durrett has built more than 50 such communities throughout the country, with many more no doubt to come.[10] Look for cohousing and housesharing to become a very common thing as boomers create communal pods that they can call home.

OPPORTUNITY

Develop products and services designed for group living situations.

ALUMNI GROUPS

Some housesharers are likely college classmates who have either stayed in touch for decades or have recently reconnected at a reunion. Strong bonds are forged at college, of course, with personal and professional relationships made during those years sometimes lasting for a lifetime. As well, college grads often have deep feelings for the institution itself that they attended even if it was decades ago, as in the case of baby boomers. Alumni associations know this better than anyone and are experts at building upon the emotional ties that graduates continue to have toward their college long after the students received their diplomas. For marketers, university alumni groups are one of the biggest communities to which anyone can belong and represent a largely overlooked, underleveraged boomerpod to consider.

The biggest and best university alumni associations are fully aware of the resource they have at their disposal and infuse their communications with the almost unlimited power of fond memories. "For those who leave Michigan, but for whom Michigan never leaves," goes the University of Michigan Alumni Association's theme line, words that resonate with many boomers who are seeking a sense of community. "As someone who walked our hallowed halls, and holds one of the most coveted diplomas in the nation, you are part of the largest living alumni body of any university anywhere," Michigan tells visitors to its website, a moving message for the hundreds of thousands of boomer Wolverines. Michigan leverages its network with bowl tour and tailgate packages, its "travel collection," and with club activities across the country and around the world, making its brand a meaningful one for those who spent some of the best years of their lives in Ann Arbor.[11]

Credit card companies like Visa and insurance companies such as Liberty Mutual are understandably partnering with alumni associations to tap into a very large market of brand loyal consumers. "Since Liberty Mutual first began working with the USC [University of Southern California] Alumni Association, we have had nothing but positive experiences," beamed Yesel Alcantar, an exec with that insurance company, adding that "we have been extremely satisfied with the partnership and the exceptional level of support received." Given the range of ways marketers can partner with the USC Alumni Association, it's not surprising that execs like Alcantar are pleased. There are direct marketing opportunities like e-newsletters to link a company's brand to that of USC in order to be part of the "extended Trojan Family," and the ability to sponsor events throughout the academic year. Marketing partners can also hook up with various groups in order to interface with business-, age-, geographic-, gender-, and other specific slices of Trojan Nation, including the Black Alumni Association, Latino Alumni Association, LAMBDA, and the LGBT Alumni Association.[12] Because they have had more time to look back and sift through the clutter of life, boomers are in general especially passionate alumni, making such partnerships more often than not a good investment of marketing dollars.

And because they are typically grounded in long-term relationships, alumni groups represent a powerful boomerpod that most marketers have oddly ignored. The travel and tourism industry gets it, however, and serves as a model for other marketers to follow. Many 60-somethings like to travel with people with whom they either know or have something in common, with college alumni serving as an ideal affinity group. The University of Utah Alumni Association has had considerable success marketing cruises to alumni, for example, as has the University of Arkansas.[13] Cornell's Alumni Association Travel Program offers Big Redders "an extraordinary journey in good company," not at all an exaggeration. (Recent trips include "Cuba: The People, Culture, & Art," "The Wolves of Yellowstone," "East Asia Crystal Cruise," and "Africa's Wildlife.")[14] Harris Made, the British maker of fine bags and accessories, has brilliantly partnered with Cornell and other American university alumni associations at Harvard, Princeton, and the University of Chicago to create bespoke, made-to-order designs bearing the respective institution's seal in order to, in the company's words, "help reinforce your traditions, heritage, values, pride, and fellowship."[15]

Northwestern University's Alumni Association (NAA) is another top marketer to boomers wishing to travel with fellow Wildcats. NAA travelers enjoy exclusive perks such as VIP status at many entertainment destinations, personalized museum tours, and edification from leading experts in a particular field. More often than not, a professor from the university who has intimate familiarity with the area hosts alumni trips, enriching the journey by providing local color with a scholarly foundation. "Best of all," the association promises, "you'll enjoy your adventure in the company of Northwestern alumni and friends," the real hook of the pitch.[16] Travelers on alumni association trips often carry school flags and are given gifts bearing their university's name, nickname, or logo— branding at its best and something that all kinds of marketers to boomers should consider.

OPPORTUNITY

Team up with alumni associations to be part of a passionate community of boomers.

MEETUPS

Pop quiz: Where can one find a community of more than 150,000 baby boomers actively looking to get together with each other? Answer: At the 540 boomer Meetups scattered around the world. Meetup.com's group gatherings provide the opportunity for boomers to connect, with events ranging from singles supper clubs to walking excursions, movies, and group yoga sessions. With almost 30 million members in over a quarter million groups in 179 countries, Meetup is a monster global community that could only have developed because of the reach of the Internet. Meetup brings people together in thousands of cities to do more of what they want to do in life, a simple but powerful proposition. Humans are at their best when they get together and do the things that matter to them, Meetup convincingly argues, delivering on its grand mission to "help people come alive."[17]

Take, for example, the "I'm Not Dead Yet" (INDY) Meetup for 50+ers in Glen Ellyn, Illinois, of which almost 5,000 boomers belong. INDYers can meet up at a variety of regular events like "Busting Boredom in the Burbs" (Glen Ellyn is a western suburb of Chicago), the "Singles & Social Club," and "TGIF" (not "Thank God It's Friday" but rather "This Group Is Fun"). Other Glen Ellyn groups include the Cook & DuPage County Trail Blazers for hikers, cyclists, and other outdoorsy enthusiasts. "Meetup for lunch and conversation in the Ginkgo Room at Morton Arboretum at 11:00 AM on Tuesday, November 8th," goes a typical post for the group, advising interested members to "Look for a long table with a Meetup sign."[18] Social media is an important part of any Meetup group, with members keeping the conversation going in between face-to-face get-togethers.

Other Meetup groups across the United States reflect not just boomers' *joie de vivre* but their communitarian roots. "Our intention is to build an active, harmonious community of interesting people by offering an abundance of diverse activities that allow our members to come together to have fun, while nurturing our minds, bodies, and spirits," states the mission of "It's Boomertime!" in Austin, Texas, with the 3,120 members of that group hoping that "this investment of time and energy will make it easier for us to open our hearts to forming new connections that lead to lasting and meaningful friendships." The South Florida Baby Boomer Meetup group is "for the young and young at heart," with its 3,000+ members declaring they "have a passion for living life to its fullest." (With karaoke night at the American Rock Bar in Deerfield Beach every Wednesday and weekly sessions of Yummy Yoga in Delray, that's no lie.) The 900 members of the North Atlanta Metro Baby Boomer Meetup Group, meanwhile, get together for game nights, Sunday brunches, movie screenings, pub quizzes, and potluck dinners, making it easy to see how such gatherings can be the foundation of a genuine social network.[19]

Even smaller Meetup groups can offer its members a meaningful sense of community. BoomerAge in Duluth, Minnesota, may have only 55 active members, for example, but the group enjoys a full calendar of fitness activities including hiking, walking, biking, tennis, pickleball, skiing, skating, rock climbing, snowshoeing, and dancing. "BoomerAge was formed to bring together adults interested in getting and staying physically fit and to promote the concept of active aging," it explains, capturing the essence of Boomers 3.0 by proclaiming, "we are committed to improving the quality of life for a new generation of seniors."[20]

While certainly the biggest aggregator of boomer get-togethers, Meetup .com is not the only game in town. Local groups offer an alternative to Meetup.com and can be more in touch with the social dynamics of a particular city. After starting out as an online social group on Meetup.com, for example, Phoenix-based Wild Boomer Women (WBW) has become a membership-based, private social club for people who, well, fit that description. "I realized I needed girlfriends to go out and have fun," said WBW founder Sue Barenholtz after getting divorced, knowing she was onto something when she put up her site on a Monday and by Friday 100 women had signed up. Much like a local Meetup group, the club meets a couple of times a week for happy hours and other events and travels together, along the way bonding over work, health, family, and relationships. "There are a lot of situations that we're all going through at the same time," Barenholtz observed, finding women of a similar age to be an essential social network for boomers like herself. Book talks (*Fifty Shades of Grey* was particularly well attended), inner tubing down the Salt River, hot air ballooning, wine tastings, and painting lessons are other activities WBW members have enjoyed. The club also hosts an annual charity event, with a recent benefit raising thousands of dollars for Bridging the Gap between Breast Cancer and Beauty.[21] The Phoenix area is quite a buzzing beehive of boomer women, with other groups like Scottsdale's Savvy Boomers and Sassy Sister also serving as vehicles of community for ladies with much in common.[22]

OPPORTUNITY

Sponsor Meetup and similar events to reach boomers at a grass-roots level.

BRAND COMMUNITIES

Ever since Thomas C. O'Guinn and Albert Muniz Jr. came up with the phrase for an article in the *Journal of Consumer Research*, the idea of a brand community has understandably become a source of fascination in the marketing world. For the authors, a brand community is "a specialized, non-geographically bound community, based on a structured set of social relations among admirers of a brand," with three main characteristics: "shared consciousness," "rituals and traditions," and "a sense of moral responsibility."[23] Pat Hong from Linkdex, a Search Engine Optimization (SEO) firm, considers such communities to be marketers' "ultimate asset," with research showing that they extend a brand's assets to more consumers and contribute to the "user journey" by building affinity and loyalty.[24]

Given the power of such a concept, it's easy to see how many marketers have spent considerable time and effort trying to turn their brands into communities. Turns out it's not so easy, however. Managers make a number of critical mistakes when it comes to brand communities, such as thinking they serve as a marketing strategy when they have wider value for an organization. Assuming a brand community represents an organization tool when it actually exists to serve people in it is another common error marketers make when trying to implement the concept. Believing that building the brand is the means to make the community follow is also the wrong path to take, as it is by engineering the community that brands are likely to become stronger. Other brand community faux pas include trying to curb the conflict inherent to any kind of group, putting too much faith in designated or self-proclaimed "opinion leaders," and relying too heavily on online social networks. While certainly useful, Facebook and Twitter messages do not effectively reach or engage audiences to the degree that brand communities can.[25]

So who is doing brand communities right, at least when it comes to marketing to boomers in their third act of life? The most obvious is the Harley Owners Group (HOG), a corporately managed organization run by Harley-Davidson for chopper devotees. The HOG was started in 1983 as a means of creating tighter, more enduring relationships with consumers when Harley-Davidson was close to going belly up. The HOG is "the granddaddy of all community-building efforts," many experts agree, as it exists not only to help market a product but, to use that overworked term, a "lifestyle."[26] The HOG has opened new revenue streams for the company through a seemingly infinite array of branded stuff available to members of the club. (My favorite is the tricked-out Fisher-Price Harley-Davidson Tough Trike.) There are more than a million Hoggers, many of them bandana-wearing boomers cruising down the road with fellow easy riders.[27]

Recipe ideas may not seem to be an ideal foundation around which to build a passionate brand community, but somehow Kraft has done just that. The company's online hub serves as a central gathering place for more traditional foodies to find recipes for regular meals or holiday menus. Cooking videos show visitors to the site how to get it done, and a blog, coupon section, nutrition information, and entertaining guide are there too. As a refrigerator and kitchen cabinet forager, I personally like the "Use What's on Hand" feature, where one can tell the Krafties what ingredients you've got laying around and they will offer meal suggestions based on that.[28] With its recipe leanings toward comfort food, potlucks, casseroles, and the like (company brands include Cool Whip, Jell-O, Miracle Whip, Velveeta, and Shake 'N Bake), Kraft's brand community might be a throwback of sorts, but its success illustrates why hipness is not an essential marketing ingredient.

Like Kraft, Sears is an old school brand that through determination and innovative thinking has built a strong community of boomer consumers. With company experts and support staff at the ready to provide answers, 1.3 million people have visited MySears Community to get help and information. Users of Sears products (appliances, clothing, and a bunch of other stuff, in case you haven't been to a store since the Nixon administration) can also start a discussion, share their ideas, or learn how to pursue a do-it-yourself project. To its credit, the struggling retailer also has a "Heroes at Home" and a "Military Employment" program and allows MySears members to donate money to help rebuild the homes of people that are either unsafe or unhealthy.[29]

Last but not least, Allstate's "Good Hands News" nicely demonstrates how a brand community can serve as a dynamic boomerpod. A wealth of information is provided in the online community's "Life at Home" area, making it a place consumers go for tips on organizing, maintaining, decorating, improving, selling, and protecting one's domicile. Articles addressing safety and security issues are mixed in with fluffier ones, a means of plugging Allstate's products and services without being overtly commercial. "On the Road" addresses vehicular considerations, while its "Money Matters" section covers financial topics. A variety of tools are offered in the "My Perks" section, more reason for community members to feel like they are in good hands.[30]

OPPORTUNITY

Create a community around your brand to offer boomers
a sense of belonging.

SOCIAL NETWORKING

What's old may indeed be new again. Millennials may have flocked to the biggest social media sites like Facebook a decade or so ago when they were new, but now boomers are flocking to them to find community. About a quarter of millennials have dropped out of Facebook over the past few years, according to a study by iStrategy Labs, while at the same time there was an 80 percent uptick in users who were 55+. Too many old folks moved in on Facebook, teens say in explaining why they have moved on to cooler, more visual sites like Pinterest, Instagram, and Snapchat, thinking there are few things creepier than discovering that one's parents, aunts and uncles, and grandparents want to Friend you (and thus learn a lot about what one is up to). "I appreciate the gesture and [older relatives'] wanting to keep up with my life, but it's kind of annoying," said one teen about the situation, something maybe Mark Zuckerberg didn't anticipate when he and his college pals created Facebook.[31] Of course, boomers are not on Facebook only to learn what's up with their kids and grandkids but to reconnect with old sweethearts, childhood friends, and former work colleagues.

With over a billion monthly users of Facebook, Zuckerberg is probably not losing sleep about some teens' decision that it has become squaresville. In fact, he should be delighted that boomers are taking their place, given that the generation represents just 25 percent of the population of the United States but owns north of 70 percent of the country's collective worth and possesses half of its purchasing power. Roughly two-thirds of American boomers are on Facebook, with LinkedIn, MyLife, Google+, and other popular online destinations. AARP's online community is more about finding people who share a common interest and having a forum to discuss issues facing older folks.[32]

A much smaller but far more close-knit online community of boomers is boomerwomenspeak.com. The website offers a different kind of social networking that is, as its name makes clear, "all about Baby Boomer women," allowing them to connect in a more personal way. At boomerwomenspeak.com, women not only connect through their interests but educate and empower one another, the thing that sets it apart. "We are the place for baby boomer women to encourage, connect, and support one another online," the site tells visitors, encouraging feelings of connectedness, acceptance, and solidarity. "We want women across the world to realize that we are not alone in our thoughts, emotions, and actions," it adds, going well beyond the usual posting of photos of grandkids on Facebook.[33]

It is the more than 60 forums of boomerwomenspeak in which women get down and dirty. Each one somehow pertains to boomer women, so users can meet new people who share their passions and interests in life. Genuine relationships are often formed, illustrating the connective power of a boomerpod. Women compare notes on caregiving, divorce, domestic violence, empty nesting, finances, illness, loss, menopause, our bodies, singlehood, step parenting, and dozens more topics, finding strength in sisterhood. The site's "Our Voices" section gives users the chance to speak their minds in a longer form and more intimate way than via typical social media. "'Our Voices' is a growing collection of fascinating stories that shares what is on the hearts and minds of women born between 1946 and 1964," we learn, with "these stories of triumph and self-discovery giving hope and inspiration to those who feel like they are alone."[34]

Giving such a voice to older women is a response to the idea that there are few outlets for people of all ages to share deep feelings with others. Laura Pappano, author of *The Connection Gap: Why Americans Feel So Alone*, maintains that our hectic pace prevents individuals from truly relating to other people, making communities like boomerwomenspeak all the more important. "We are never alone on this roller coaster ride called LIFE," said founder Dotsie Bregel, firm in her belief that "women need the opportunity to share personal stories that will touch the hearts and souls of our generation and help us feel connected."[35] Some users have decided to meet in person after sharing their online friendship, illustrating how much the site is valued by users.

Bregel was not just the founder of boomerwomenspeak but also the National Association of Baby Boomer Women (NABBW), which devotes most of its energy toward supporting female boomers in various ways. The NABBW is "passionately dedicated to uniting, supporting, advocating for, and educating baby boomer women throughout the world," it legitimately claims, offering a diverse menu of services and perks for its members. Moreover, the NABBW aims to be a close ally with its global membership with the intent of improving women's overall quality of life—something much needed in many parts of the world. Committed to "friendship, personal integrity, service to others, personal excellence and intellectual pursuits, community involvement, and personal and career development," the NABBW is an important boomerpod that marketers should not overlook. "We are women—sisters, daughters, mothers, wives and friends—who are inspired by our values to serve the world," reads the vision of the organization, words that should inspire us all.[36]

OPPORTUNITY

Connect with women boomers by allowing them to connect with each other.

EIGHT

Gray Power

The old are becoming the new new thing.

The Economist, 2016

No, "gray" and "power" are not oxymoronic terms. Boomers may be turning gray but their social and economic power is intensifying, proving that older age can be a time of strength and resiliency. This chapter, Gray Power, riffs on the Black Power movement of the late 1960s, when more militant African Americans formed an ideology based on forceful activism and empowerment. While age-based discrimination is not nearly as malevolent as that based on race, it is very real and serves as a debilitating force for millions of Americans in their mid-fifties and up. Boomers are on the cusp of becoming a recognized constituency in their third act of life, however, building on the efforts of seniors of past generations who made their presence known in order to shape public policy.

Boomers are unlike past generations in every imaginable way, however, making Gray Power a different sort of beast than previous such movements. A major component of Gray Power is the political clout of boomers, which I believe will coalesce in the years ahead—a reasonable assumption given that the group is sure to represent a major voting bloc for any elected official or candidate regardless of party. Millions of boomers with both the time and money (many of them lawyers) will exert great influence on the nation's political and economic landscape, seeing the effort as their last opportunity to shape the country's future. Although ageism will be just part of this activism, Gray Power can potentially give older people the respect and fair treatment they deserve, being analogous in some respects to previous large-scale movements by marginalized groups, for example, civil rights, feminism, and gay rights.

Boomers' best chance of defeating ageism is through their economic power. Boomers' collective wealth is an underutilized resource, as through their spending power they have the ability to motivate Corporate America to stop ageist practices that typically go unreported. Given their activist roots, boomers have been remarkably passive in this regard to date, something that I believe will change in the near future. Through the kind of boomerpods described in the last chapter, boomers will form alliances that will allow them to exert their Gray Power. Boomers will also be a visible force in the workplace, healthcare system, and suburban communities, ignoring the many younger people who wish they would just go away after dominating American society for so long.

So how do marketers fit into this paradigm of Gray Power? Aligning with boomers as their power consolidates over the next two decades is a smart strategy for virtually any kind of business, as the group is sure to be both an economic powerhouse and a key political lobby or coalition. As well, many marketers have already abandoned boomers as consumers, wrongly assuming they do not like to switch brands or spend money. Other marketers want their brands to be youthful and conclude that associating with boomers would be off-strategy. Such thinking is both shortsighted and misguided, ignoring the fact that boomers are the same force of nature they have always been.

OPPORTUNITY

Be an advocate for Gray Power in every arena possible.

GRAY RIGHTS

Four decades after the Gay Rights movement peaked, the Gray Rights movement is at last hitting its stride. It's ironic that baby boomers—the generation that also protested the Vietnam War, fought for racial justice, and pursued gender equality in the 1960s and 1970s—have waited so long to confront widespread discrimination against themselves. Boomers are increasingly the target of ageism ("thinking or believing in a negative manner about the process of becoming old or about old people"), a likely by-product of a culture in which getting older is often seen as having little or no positive value.

A little history of ageism helps put today's battle for Gray Rights in context. It was legendary physician and gerontologist Robert Butler who coined the term in 1969 to describe individuals who faced discrimination and prejudice because they were considered old. Butler had observed the lack of respect shown to the elderly and their conditions in medical school, a theme that heavily informed his 1975 book *Why Survive? Being Old in America*. The book was a scathing indictment on ageism in America, detailing how older people were consistently socially excluded and routinely taken advantage of. Butler argued that it was up to older Americans themselves to adopt the kind of militancy that other oppressed groups had done. Voter registration drives, marches, and whistle-blowing were all things seniors could do to strike back against the virulent form of discrimination that was engrained in American society.[1]

The 1978 anthology *The New Old: Struggling for Decent Aging* also served as a kind of manifesto for older Americans. Seniors were treated shamefully, that book argued; its contributors made a compelling case that ageism was the last form of segregation in the nation. As with *Why Survive?*, the book also included an agenda for action, urging that older people stand up for their rights. The formation of the Gray Panthers in 1970 (whose name was inspired by the militant Black Panthers) was another attempt to dispel stereotypes about older people and to influence legislature affecting them. Activism by that group (which is still around) was centered around the "three Hs"—health, hunger, and housing—with much of it directed at the Ford administration's budget cutting as it dismantled a good part of LBJ's "Great Society" programs.[2]

Now, with tens of millions of boomers facing discrimination on a daily basis, the time is ripe to defeat ageism once and for all via a full-fledged Gray Rights movement. Conquering America's worship of youth and contempt of aging has become the mission of a number of contemporary gerontologists and geriatricians, notably Bill Thomas. Thomas, a geriatrician and the author of *What Are Old People For?* and *Second Wind: Navigating the Passage to a Slower, Deeper, and More Connected Life*, is a passionate ambassador for older people; his goal is to change the perception of aging from a medical condition to a natural stage of life. "Elderhood," as Thomas referred to the second half of life, should receive more respect in American society, a message he delivered to audiences in 30 cities on his 2015 "Age of Disruption" tour.[3]

Thanks to Thomas and others, the idea of elderhood is indeed taking hold. If childhood is the first stage of human development and adulthood the second, elderhood is the third, a time of life finally getting the attention and respect it deserves. As part of the conscious aging movement discussed in Chapter 6, more New Age boomers are getting together in "circles" to celebrate elderhood. "Elder circles are cropping up across the nation with a focus on helping older people learn how to get rid of negative thoughts about aging, and instead frame it in a positive way that includes an expanded consciousness and wisdom," observed Rose Caiola, founder of RewireMe.com, adding that elders are also "giving back to community and society by sharing their wisdom with the younger generation."[4]

Boomers don't have to buy into the concept of conscious aging or call themselves elders to demand Gray Rights, however. Bias against individuals because of their age is as "pernicious as racism, sexism, or discrimination against people with disabilities, or any other prejudice," says Seattle-based IlluminAge Communication Partners, yet it remains widely accepted (and, in some cases, such as in the tech industry, actually encouraged). Ageism is expressed as (illegal) unfairness directed to older people via non-truthful categorizations, and often in outright antagonism and umbrage to individuals not deemed to be "young." Moreover, ageism is not just morally wrong but actually bad for one's health: intolerance based on age frequently leads to both emotional and physical damage for its victims, who now include baby boomers.[5]

Fortunately, more and more boomers are returning to their activist roots by wielding Gray Power, a function of the seismic shift that is taking place in the nation's population. (By the mid-2030s, the 65+ population will be twice what it is now, increasing from 35 million citizens to more than 70 million, according to the U.S. Administration on Aging.) "Today we are seeing efforts on the individual, institutional, national and global fronts that aim to fight ageism and impress on everyone that every stage of life is valuable," IlluminAge continues, good news for boomers' third act of life.[6]

OPPORTUNITY

Join the cause as the Gray Rights movement accelerates.

GRAY POLITICS

At about a third of the electorate, baby boomers eclipse other generational groups, something they've done since the late 1970s when most reached voting age. Boomers' political leanings are generally bipartisan, not surprising given their diversity across class, race, and gender lines. Older people tend to be avid voters, however, making many think boomers will form a powerful political bloc in the years ahead. Some are concerned that this bloc will be centered around "senior" issues that protect or expand their interests at the cost of those of younger people who are paying most of the taxes. Older voters of the past have lobbied to preserve Social Security and Medicare, not surprisingly, something that will no doubt continue as these entitlements are threatened by future budget-cutting politicians.[7]

The likelihood that boomers will represent a political force with which to reckon for a couple more decades is great given the fact that they are also still running for office. With the election of Gen Xer Barack Obama in 2008, many assumed that boomers were ready to leave politics en masse and make room for younger candidates. The battle for president in 2016 between two boomers—Donald Trump and Hillary Clinton—proved that assumption wrong, however, and there are many 60-somethings in other political positions who have no intention of stepping down because of their age.[8] Politics is turning out to be a popular second or encore career among boomers who have moved on from their first. Lawyers in particular are entering the political arena after their career track stalls or they decide to opt out of the private sector. Many politicians have law degrees, of course, making the transition to becoming a mayor or other city official not too difficult, given their experience of working in the system.[9]

Given the number of positions to fill, it's not surprising that boomers are jumping into politics in significant numbers (despite their well documented distrust of government as young adults). There are more than 18,000 people in office in state legislatures and another 320,000 positions in local government. Still more people are needed for the country's 180,000 school and special district posts, however, with boomers often taking those jobs. While there might be some irony in boomers becoming elected officials when they would once be found in a politician's office only because they were staging a sit-in, the phenomenon can be seen as an extension of their activist roots. "Baby boomers are a generation of amateur enthusiasts for political causes," argued Neil Howe, an expert in demographics and the head of Great Falls, Virginia-based LifeCourse Associates, a consultancy, in explaining why so many are taking these jobs.[10] Many boomers dreamed of changing the system from the inside but got diverted into other fields, making this a kind of coming full circle.

Professors who have left academia after many years are also entering politics, as are businesspeople looking for a new challenge. Positions are often part-time, perfect for those folks who would be reluctant to take on another 40-hour (or more) workweek. Money is often not the motive, as the salaries for mayors and state legislators are typically small. (Many staff members are actually unpaid volunteers.) As well, unlike many younger politicians, relatively few boomers have ambitions to get elected to higher office. Those with business experience find it to be a valuable asset in the political arena, something the president of the United States made clear when he ran for office. Simply having been around the block a few times also helps out in politics. "More experience in life qualifies you for making wise decisions," observed 90-year-old Betty Taylor, an elected official in Eugene, Oregon, having no plans at all to retire.[11]

While boomers' entering politics later in life makes perfect sense given their commitment to positive social change, it is once again AARP members who as a lobby can shape legislation for the good. For over a half century, in fact, AARP has been a loud voice championing the rights of older Americans. AARP's mission in this regard is to improve each of our lives as we get older by providing knowledge, resources, and support. The organization "believes strongly in the principles of collective purpose, collective voice, and collective purchasing power," it proudly states, all things that will help make boomers a powerful constituency in the years ahead. AARP's noble vision—"a society in which everyone ages with dignity and purpose"—is ideally aligned with boomers' quest to fulfill their goals and dreams in their third act of life. AARP is an activist at all levels of government, with its Advocacy Program focused on those matters that are most relevant to older Americans. AARP then communicates vital intelligence regarding those subjects to enable its constituency to chime in. AARPers who take part in its Advocacy Program often make phone calls or send e-mails to elected officials, and are sometimes invited to conferences or have direct contact with them (the latter usually after circulating a petition). Whether the issue is healthcare, government entitlements, housing, or something else, AARP's Advocacy Program ensures that politicians hear members' voices.[12]

OPPORTUNITY

Lobby for boomers as they form an increasingly powerful political bloc.

GRAY MARKET

Again, boomers' greatest weapon in stopping ageism is by putting their money where their mouth is. Ever since boomers were tots, marketers have chased them as consumers, knowing that's where the action was. Boomers still spend the most money in the marketplace, both in this country and globally, but marketers are no longer sure what kind of products and service to create for them or how to talk to them. Stereotypes related to "oldness," such as that people in their sixties have little interest in shopping, except for things used by "old" people, persist despite much evidence to the contrary. The fact that most marketing people at Fortune 500 companies are Gen Xers or millennials doesn't help matters, as they tend to see the world through a youthful lens. Companies have found that treating boomers as a kind of special interest group demanding different kinds of products and services just because they are not young anymore is a big mistake, making marketing to boomers a major challenge.

Still, "change is in the air," according to a recent story on the gray economy in *The Economist*, with that magazine declaring, "older consumers will reshape the business landscape." Marketers in many industries, including healthcare, autos, retailing, and consumer goods, are leading what has been called the "silver rush," excited about what represents one of the few major growth opportunities in the global economy. Emerging markets have not turned out to be the bonanza many were hoping they would be, and millennials have yet to become enthusiastic consumers in big-ticket categories like real estate and cars. Millennials famously like to keep their options open and understandably want to avoid taking on additional debt. (The more than 40 million of them who borrowed money to pay for school are as a group $1.3 trillion+ in the hole, with the average graduate owing $30,000–$40,000.)[13]

One thus does not have to be a business genius to know that it makes more sense to devote more resources marketing to a generation deservedly known as professional consumers than one that is highly selective about how they spend money. Marketers like Kimberly-Clark and Ford have joined the silver rush, with many more planning to do so but not quite sure how to go about it. "You'd have to be an idiot to turn your back on this humongous growth market," quipped Jody Holtzman, director of AARP's Thought Leadership division, back in 2013, an interesting observation given how few companies are currently targeting older consumers. Venture capitalists have also to-date ignored the gray economy, apparently thinking it's just not as sexy as another tech start-up. The myths that older consumers are resistant to new brand experiences or are saving their money for retirement have contributed to the myopia, and efforts to try to segment the market into traditionally defined demographic groups have not surprisingly failed.[14]

No single marketer is currently taking the boomer market more seriously and thoughtfully than Procter & Gamble. In partnership with the University of Cincinnati, P&G has founded Live Well Collaborative (LWC), a nonprofit dedicated to the growing need for design solutions for boomers. The mission of the LWC is to develop breakthrough innovations for consumers across their lifespan, with the organization claiming to have successfully completed over 50 projects in a wide variety of industries. Whether or not these projects have actually reached the market, it cannot be argued that LWC is an expert in the boomer market and continues to expand its portfolio by partnering with healthcare institutions.[15]

If boomers as a whole are being undermarketed to given their numbers and collective wealth, boomer women are being virtually ignored by Corporate America. While beauty and fashion marketers aggressively pursue teenage girls and young women and makers of consumer products have a lovefest with moms, few companies seem interested in women over 50. (Avon, Target, Amazon, Olay, Cadillac, L'Oreal, Dove, and Eileen Fisher are notable exceptions, as a recent survey conducted by Girlpower Marketing pointed out.) This is odd, of course, as many boomer women now have the time and money to invest in themselves. Just do the math: boomers accounted for about $230 billion in CPG revenues in 2012 (almost half of that year's aggregate sales), according to a Nielsen study done that year, and females account for three-quarters of all spending. "Most of the female baby boomers feel as if marketers don't really understand them, and they're not making a really strong, concerted effort to speak to them as individuals," said Dave Austin of Influent50, a part of AARP Services.[16]

Although most marketers have so far been reluctant to prioritize boomers, especially those who happen to be women, it's important to remember that the gray economy has a long way to go. Savvier marketers will figure out how to best pitch boomers in their third act of life, just as they did in their first and second. "This is only the early stages of a revolution," *The Economist* concludes, correctly observing that "baby-boomers have spent their lives making noise and demanding attention and they are not going to stop now."[17]

OPPORTUNITY
Get in early on the silver rush to make your fortune.

GRAY WORKPLACE

"Baby boomers still got game in their life and work," declares Ira Wolfe of Success Performance Solutions, explaining why many millennials have hit the "gray ceiling"—the challenge for young people to climb up the corporate ladder. Experts' predictions that boomers would go gently into that good night of retirement have been wrong; the older American workforce is close to a historic high, up by about 33 percent in 25 years. A number of factors—a gradually increasing employment rate, longer life expectancy, and the fact that boomers simply like to work and can use the money—have wreaked havoc with the traditional pattern of older workers hanging up their hats to make room for younger ones.[18] The result has been not a loss but a gain in Gray Power, something in which youth-obsessed marketers may want to heed.

Workers used to count the days to their 65th birthday, the traditional age of retirement, but that is much less true today. Besides being more active than prior generations, the (current) rules of Social Security are a strong incentive to wait to collect benefits until age 70. Monthly checks are 32 percent higher for those who keep working four years past the full retirement age of 66, a juicy carrot to dangle. Many boomers are thus thinking 70 may be a good age to stop working, but no one really knows if or when they will call it a day. Again, "unretirement" is now at least as popular as retirement for boomers, a phenomenon that is altering the landscape of the American workplace.[19]

Boomers' refusal to budge from their jobs can be seen in the numbers. The American workforce is getting decidedly grayer: 22.2 percent of workers are over the age of 55, according to a 2014 Bureau of Labor Statistics report, the highest it has ever been. That part of the labor force aged 55 or older increased by 3.5 million between 2009 and 2012, the *Wall Street Journal* reported, making boomers a visible presence in most offices. The average age of the United States Senate is 62, a prime example of the gray workplace. While Gen Xers and millennials might wish that boomers would sail off into the sunset so that they could occupy what are often plum positions in senior management, unretirement is actually good for the nation's economy. Once (or if) boomers stop working, they will begin drawing on Social Security and Medicare—benefits that are already running at a deficit and are forecast to go broke by 2033.[20]

While boomers have a number of good reasons to keep working, the decision often comes down to one thing: money and healthcare benefits. Pensions have shrunk at many companies, and the fear of another major recession like the one in 2008 shriveling up one's nest egg is motivation enough to stay at one's job as long as possible. "Money—or the lack of it—coupled with a desire to continue living the good life (and paying the bills associated with it) is the number one driver of prolonged Boomer work," wrote Robert McGarvey in thestreet.com in 2016, with an alarming number of boomers having no retirement savings at all.[21] A 20- or 30-year retirement is not just a lot of time to fill but is an expensive proposition, especially given the greater healthcare needs that are likely to arrive sooner or later. Another reason to remain a nine-to-fiver is that one's spouse isn't ready for a life of leisure or, perhaps, isn't particularly excited about their husband or wife puttering around their house all day wondering what he or she should be doing with all that newfound time.

One other factor for boomers' determination to still show up everyday for work is the feeling that they have not completed a certain goal. Knowing that one may have regrets about stopping short of an important achievement is a powerful inducement to not call it quits until that mission is accomplished, whether that means selling one's company, introducing a product or service to market, or any number of other objectives. Making a dream come true—especially if that dream was decades in the making—is a good reason to stay in the game, even if one has other dreams that have nothing to do with work.

If one needed yet more justification to put off going fishing or some other leisurely equivalent, it's that there is solid research indicating that a mostly passive life is bad for one's health (particularly for Alpha types). Paid employment and volunteer work each provide individuals with a strong sense of purpose and meaning, one of the keys to mental and physical health. Jobs that offer social interaction, such as Uber driving, too contribute a sense of well-being. In fact, more Uber drivers today are older than 50 than younger than 30, a sign that boomers are not prioritizing retirement in their third act of life, even if they could afford to do so. Full retirement is, in short, a health risk, an idea that is completely contrary to the view held a half century ago when boomers were in knee pants. Whether one is still engaged in one's first, original career or is embarking on a second or encore career, remaining productive through some kind of job is a supporting factor for a longer, happier life. "The baby boomer generation has lived through decades of radical political and social change, so it should be no surprise that they are also revolutionizing retirement," George Lorenzo of *Fast Company* observed, astute analysis that supports the argument of ascending Gray Power.[22]

> **OPPORTUNITY**
>
> Don't assume boomers are in retirement mode and
> saving their pennies.

GRAY HEALTHCARE

One may think of baby boomers as a healthy and fit generation, the result of being gym rats during the Reagan administration. While there are indeed many boomers who are fit as a fiddle, the reality is that the generation as a whole has some major health issues despite smoking a lot less than the greatest generation. Obesity, diabetes, hypertension, and high cholesterol are common, ailments that often lead to chronic conditions such as heart disease. Boomers grew up in the age of television and then the personal computer, technologies that encouraged a sedentary lifestyle. America became a fast-food nation just as boomers became young adults, a less than healthy diet that has led to physical problems down the road. Mental health is also not a pretty picture; boomers have relatively high rates of depression, anxiety disorders, and substance abuse, perhaps because there is now more openness about seeking treatment for such illnesses. Finally, stress has become the malady du jour, not a good recipe to maintain good physical or mental health.

Given all that, why do many boomers think of themselves as generally healthy people and maintain an active lifestyle not all that different from when they were 30 or 40? The answer is that boomers are as a rule optimistic and bent on looking and feeling young, a literally healthy way of approaching life. Aging is not just physical, geriatric psychiatrists point out, with a psychosocial element playing a key role in shaping one's personal health. Being and staying positive becomes a self-fulfilling prophecy, with those getting caught up in the negative aspects of aging more likely to get sick and die earlier.

While embracing rather than denying the entirely natural process of getting older is good for one's health, there's no getting around the fact that tens of millions of boomers will eventually develop the physical conditions that typically come with age. Because of this, boomers will alter the landscape of healthcare in this country as well, with a shift in resources dedicated to medicine for older people. "This is the most powerful force operating in our health system right now, this generational change," stated Jeff Goldsmith, the head of Health Futures Inc. of Charlottesville, Virginia, seeing the aging of boomers as the most significant issue for both caregivers and policy makers for decades to come. Precision or customized medicine is one of the bigger changes already in progress, especially as related to cancer treatment. Each patient and tumor is considered unique in the emerging field of genomics, something in which boomers will benefit. Besides more targeted, less toxic chemotherapies, holistic medicine approaches such as acupuncture are becoming more readily accepted among Western physicians.[23]

There are a host of other new developments in the healthcare industry geared specifically to the aging boomer market. Geriatric emergency departments that are designed for boomers and seniors, such as the one at UC San Diego Health, in a partnership with West Health, is one of them, and mobile health—a 21st-century version of the housecall, where medical guidance is given to the patient without requiring an office visit—is another. The chronic care system is likely to be overhauled with the arrival of boomers, as older people tend to have more than one condition, something not very well addressed by the current system. Slowing the epidemic of Alzheimer's disease and dementia is perhaps the biggest challenge and opportunity in the world of gray healthcare, with many clinical trials taking place right now to try to do just that.[24]

All of this can't be done without people, however, and many of them. The current number of healthcare workers is insufficient to manage the graying of America, with a vast shortage predicted if things don't change. There are simply too few physicians, nurses, health and personal care aides, and other medical professionals who possess the necessary abilities to tend to the older population of the not-so-distant future. By 2020, 1.6 million such positions will be needed, and many more by 2030, with nowhere near that number in the pipeline today. Original, better designed approaches to healthcare as well as technological advancements will ease some of the greater demand for medical services for boomers, but there will still be a big gap unless something is done, and soon.[25]

The solution? True to form, it's all about the economy. Geriatric medicine is going to become not just a big part of the healthcare industry but a major chunk of the American economy, I predict, as the public and private sector band together in an unprecedented partnership. Boomers are going to wield their full gray power to stay healthy as long as possible, using both their political and economic clout to make the system adapt to their needs. As the wealthiest generation in history, boomers will pay big money for things that matter to them, with health their number one priority. Allured by high salaries, partly subsidized by the government through Medicare or another agency, job seekers will flock to the field, I believe, making healthcare work a far more lucrative and valued occupation than it is today. "BoomerCare" will recall FDR's New Deal or LBJ's Great Society, a works program that will be historic in both scope and magnitude.

OPPORTUNITY

Play a part in the emerging BoomerCare industry.

GRAY SUBURBS

Many baby boomers swore they would never return to the suburbs after having grown up there, but that prediction, like many others they made in the 1960s and 1970s about having anything to do with bourgeois society, turned out to be wrong. A good number of boomers settled down in the 'burbs to raise families after going to college and getting a dose of city life, much like their parents had done. Now, even with their kids having flown the coop, they are reluctant to leave, feeling comfortable in their house and neighborhood and with friends nearby. Some more affluent empty nesters are indeed relocating to the urban hipstervilles described in Chapter 3, but others want (or need) to age "in place," as the saying goes, with relatively few planning to move to a retirement community just because they have reached a certain age. Contrary to popular belief, older people simply don't move that much, partly because they can't afford to. (Nine in 10 older Americans want to stay in their homes as they age, according to AARP.) There are now twice as many suburban residents aged 65 or older than there were in 1950, but this is just the beginning of graying of the 'burbs.[26]

The prospect of suburbia—the outer ring of cities purposely designed to be child-friendly—becoming a haven for older folks has huge social and economic implications. "The graying of suburbia is going to become the central challenge of the country," noted Lawrence Levy of Hofstra

University's National Center for Suburban Studies, with most of these communities not at all ready for what's coming. Suburbs are car-centric, for one thing, and multilevel houses with narrow sidewalks are not ideal for the needs of an older population. The even bigger issue is how communities decide to portion out their resources between school-age kids and seniors, with some experts thinking a major conflict is looming. Boomers who readily paid school taxes when their own kids were enrolled are now lobbying for greater senior services, exemption from school taxes and more accessible transit systems. A study by the American Public Transportation Association ball-parked that money going toward public transportation must be 81 percent greater ($8.6 billion) by 2030 given the number of boomers intending to age in place, just one of many potential economic battles to come.[27]

Many boomers today might not want to be caught dead on a bus, but flash forward 20 years, and things will be a lot different. Assuming cars cannot completely safely drive by themselves by then, basic activities like getting groceries or getting to a doctor's appointment will be difficult. And with bedrooms and full bathrooms on second floors, the typical houses built during the postwar boom were clearly not conceived with 80-year-olds in mind. Suburbia is also low-density, meaning people are spread out over a relatively large area. Isolation—one of the worst things that can happen to an older person—is thus a strong possibility based on the current design of the suburbs, another reason why changes have to be made if boomers are determined to stay put. Public transportation, home retrofitting, and visiting services take money, of course, and are thus things that millennials are understandably not excited about paying for.[28]

Hopefully, some equitable balance can be struck between aging boomers and millennials wanting to start their own families in the suburbs. The healthiest communities tend to multigenerational, after all, meaning it's in the best interests of everyone to find a good solution. But unlike seniors of the past, who were often treated unfairly like other marginalized groups, boomers are going to exert their gray power to protect their interests. "The people who show up at local government meetings are going to be the boomers," explained John McIlwain, author of *Housing in America*, this generation not reluctant to "push for what they want." Seniors in the Sun Belt have actually been exercising their gray power for some time now, but this is likely to become a larger, national phenomenon over the next couple of decades. "Boomers aging in the suburbs may use their considerable political muscle—buttressed by their numbers, relatively high education level and economic power—to transform the communities where they grew up," Jenni Bergal wrote in pewtrusts.org in 2016.[29]

So how exactly will boomers change the suburbs? Joseph Coughlin, who leads the MIT AgeLab, forecasts that baby boomers are going to push for things such as an online transportation network and subsidized technologies for home safety. In Amherst, New York, outside Buffalo, there is already a food delivery service and a youth program that hires teenagers to mow the lawns of and do maintenance work for older folks, precisely the kind of thing that is likely to become standard across the country. While the government will play a key role in this, it is the private sector—urban planners, architectural firms, healthcare companies, and retailers—that will be more motivated to take action to improve the quality of life for aging boomers. With residential housing, outdoor public spaces, brick-lined streets, common spaces, office spaces, restaurants and retail shops for use by people of all ages, mixed-use communities like Winter Park Village, Florida, and Kentlands, Maryland, serve as models for the boomer-friendly suburbs of the future.[30]

OPPORTUNITY

Find boomers in suburbia as it turns grayer.

NINE

Pay It Forward

When someone does you a big favor, don't pay it back . . . Pay It Forward.
                                    Tagline for the 2000 film *Pay It Forward*

Not that long ago for millions of Americans, reaching one's sixties meant a retirement party and then a cushy life in Florida or some other warm place. That model has imploded over the past generation or so, as those entering their third act of life chose more ambitious pursuits than water aerobics and canasta. Today, baby boomers are altering the fundamental concept of seniority, a function of living longer and the steep cost of doing so. One more factor is making boomers' later years different from those of any previous generation: their "deep-seated desire to make a difference," as Dan Kadlec, coauthor of *A New Purpose*, described it.[1] Rather than feel that retirement was payback for a lifetime of hard work, boomers see unretirement as an ideal time of life to pay it forward, flipping the idea of older age on its head.

This chapter, Pay It Forward, recognizes the good karma associated with helping others if one can in one's third act of life. Giving back is already becoming a principal activity among boomers, specifically some form of passing on what one has learned in life so far. Offering expertise in a particular area to a younger generation or others in need can be an immensely rewarding experience, and lead to a feeling of completion or coming full circle. Paying it forward will become much more structured and organized in the years ahead, I foresee, with millions of boomers to soon be looking for a new mission in life offering meaning and purpose.

Kadlec, along with aging expert Ken Dychwald, the coauthor of *A New Purpose*, have a keen sense of why boomers want to pay it forward and how they are likely to do so. After exiting one's first career, 60-somethings might take some time to enjoy the good life, whether that means travelling, visiting grandkids, or pursuing a particular passion. Soon, however, it becomes apparent that there is still a long road ahead, and lowering one's golf handicap by a few strokes is not as rewarding an achievement as it might have once seemed. Members of a generation trained to accomplish great things in life need a compelling reason to get up in the morning, which is where paying it forward comes in. In their book, Kadlec and Dychwald employ the phrase "going from success to significance" to explain the shift from an emphasis on making money to becoming an agent of change. "The idea is to find a pastime with intrinsic rewards," Kadlec wrote in *Time* in 2013, with any number of options available to making that happen. For many, giving back "is what the new model is all about," he explained, a more communitarian undertaking than the personally defined endeavors of working and raising a family.[2] There actually may be a biological component to the urge to pay it forward; some of the greatest psychologists of the 20th century, including Abraham Maslow and Eric Erikson, have argued that humans are hardwired to give back in their later years, part of the evolutionary process. Taking the initiative by creating a resource by which boomers can pay it forward would be a wise move for organizations, I believe, as giving back in some way will represent a big part of their lives until they are simply no longer able to do so.

OPPORTUNITY

Build in the concept of pay it forward into your organization's DNA.

VOLUNTEERMATCH

For nonprofits, the graying of America represents a windfall in scope and magnitude. Older people tend to volunteer in high numbers, something that is likely to hold true for boomers given their roots in social conscience. Not just the generation's size but boomers' relative health, wealth, and education level are reasons for the nonprofit world to be excited about the prospect of so many potential volunteers looking for a way to give back.[3] While they might have justifiably been called the "me generation" in the 1970s, today boomers volunteer more than any other generation, according to the Corporation for National and Community Service. Boomers are also more likely to volunteer than did previous generations, more reason to expect great things from them in the coming years.[4]

There are any number of ways for boomers to find a cause for which to volunteer, but none more seamless than VolunteerMatch. VolunteerMatch is the most popular online network of volunteers, with more than 110,000 active nonprofit organizations, 150 partnerships, and over 13 million visitors annually. The organization's mission is simple: Make it easy "for good people and good causes to connect." More than a million community-oriented individuals interested in volunteering their time for a worthwhile cause use the site, explaining why so many organizations across the country rely on it to find good people. VolunteerMatch is the favorite volunteering recruitment hub for many nonprofit organizations in the United States and provides the greatest number of results in online search engines for the term "volunteer." The organization's clout is reflected by its stable of corporate partners, which include ADT, Bank of the West, Charles Schwab, Choice Hotels International, Gap, JetBlue, Johnson & Johnson, Morgan Stanley, Nationwide, Office Depot, Robert Half, Target, and UnionBank.[5]

To its credit, VolunteerMatch recognizes the impact baby boomers are destined to have on the volunteering landscape of America. "The aging of America is likely to be the biggest demographic story of our times," observed John Gomperts, president of Civic Ventures (now Encore.org) between 2006 and 2010 and now president & CEO of America's Promise Alliance, keenly aware that over the next couple of decades boomers "will bring profound changes to schools and universities, health care and housing, the workplace and civil society, and to virtually every institution in our lives." A study cosponsored by Encore.org and the MetLife Foundation reported that many baby boomers wish to embark on a new stage in their professional life that allows the opportunity to contribute to society in an impactful way. Individuals older than 50 years of age said they were very interested in seguing from their demanding work lives to take on new challenges that bettered the quality of life for other people. Rather than seeking "busy work," boomers are searching for meaningful activities, specifically those that address major social issues such as poverty. "With knowledge and investment we can transform the aging of the baby boom generation from a potential crisis into an historic opportunity," Gomperts envisioned, seeing "millions of talented, experienced Americans ready to roll up their sleeves."[6]

Baby boomers already comprise a large percentage of VolunteerMatch volunteers, in part because there is such a wide range of opportunities from which to choose. With 58,000 opportunities and over 75,000 participating organizations, VolunteerMatch is to volunteering as Match .com is to dating. Nonprofits, schools, and other types of community organizations first register on volunteermatch.com and then post their opportunities (for free), with volunteers able to search by cause, location, and other criteria. If a volunteer is interested in a particular opportunity, the organization is notified and able to respond directly through the website. Opportunities can be found in virtually every city in the United States, with the top 10 cause areas being "Arts & Culture," "Children & Youth," "Community," "Disabled," "Education & Literacy," "Environment," "Health & Medicine," "Homeless & Housing," "International," and "Seniors." Volunteer skills include tutoring, childcare, mentoring, literacy and reading, youth services, crafts, general education, and office management.[7]

Beyond serving as the leading connector between nonprofits and volunteers, VolunteerMatch is a loud supporter of corporate volunteerism or what it calls "cross-sector" partnerships or collaborations. At its VM Summit—VolunteerMatch's annual conference on corporate volunteerism that brings nonprofits and companies together in the same room—awards are given to companies that "go above and beyond" in encouraging employee volunteerism as evidenced by high rates of engagement. (Humana and Hagerty Insurance were winners in 2016.) An award is also given to a nonprofit that excels at supporting volunteer recruitment at the local level by providing a range of opportunities including hands-on and skills-based volunteering. (The Girl Scouts won that award in 2016.) One final award recognizes the companies and organizations that have made the most connections to volunteer opportunities via the VolunteerMatch Network, with the 2016 winners being Delta, Humana, JetBlue, Raytheon, and Tulsa Community College.[8]

OPPORTUNITY

Win boomers' brand loyalty by championing corporate volunteering.

MENTOR

"Somehow we have to get older people back close to growing children if we are to restore a sense of community, a knowledge of the past and a sense of the future," said the anthropologist Margaret Mead, an idea many baby boomers are beginning to embrace. Professionals concerned about the millions of young people in the United States who are growing up in adverse circumstances are viewing boomers as a largely untapped resource which can enhance the lives of individuals and strengthen communities across the country. Mentoring is one form of volunteering designed to meet the needs of high-risk youth, as positive adult support is known to be a powerful force in any society. With a lifetime of experience in work and, often, family caregiving, boomers are ideally equipped to serve as mentors, especially given their sense of what psychologist Erik Erikson called "generativity"—the inherent human interest in guiding the next generation. Part of JFK's dream was to mobilize significant numbers of older adults by creating meaningful opportunities for service like mentoring, something only now being realized through the magic of the Internet. Boomers are seeking the chance to contribute to their communities, remain connected to others, and maintain their vitality, all things that make them excellent candidates for mentoring.[9]

No organization more than MENTOR is matchmaking boomers with mentoring. MENTOR'S vision is that "every young person has the supportive relationships he or she needs to grow and develop into thriving, productive, and engaged adults," mentoring.org explains, with its mission being to "fuel the quality and quantity of mentoring relationships for America's young people and to close the 'mentoring gap.'" One-third of kids and teens lack those kind of supportive relationships, MENTOR claims, a statistic entirely believable given the epidemic of fatherlessness in the United States.[10]

MENTOR (formally the National Mentoring Partnership) is the strongest advocate of advancing the mentoring of young people in this country, a position it has held since 1990. For more than a quarter century, MENTOR has led the mentoring way by championing the cause, creating the means to make it happen on a national basis and taking a leadership role in factually demonstrating its value. Developing and supporting a group of affiliated partners that operate at a more grass-roots level and providing the tools and resources required to increase the number of qualified mentors is another of MENTOR's key initiatives. The organization engages with both the government and corporations to make sure that young people benefit from the kind of relationships that typically lead to personal and professional success. By putting millions of at-risk youth together with responsible older adults, MENTOR's efforts have paid off. MENTOR is listed on the Social Impact 100 (S&I 100 Index), meaning it is considered one of the country's most productive nonprofits.[11]

What exactly do mentors try to achieve? In ideal circumstances, mentoring shows kids and teens that another person is emotionally invested in their welfare, makes it clear that they do not have to solve problems by themselves, and, most important, serves as primary evidence that their lives are important. Studies prove that qualified mentors are helpful to mentees in all kinds of ways. At its best, mentoring enables a child or teenager to achieve his or her full potential, something that typically leads to a more fulfilling and productive life. The results can be seen in the numbers: young adults who were at-risk for getting into some kind of trouble but were in a mentoring relationship are 55 percent more likely to go to college. As well, there is a 78 percent greater chance that mentees will volunteer on a regular basis, and a 130 percent greater chance that they will become some kind of leader. Best of all perhaps, 90 percent are interested in becoming a mentor themselves, a classic example of the ripple effect of paying it forward.[12]

While good mentors come in many different stripes, all should be empathic and respectful people and have a genuine interest in sharing a relationship with a kid or teen. Being a good listener and possessing the ability to solve problems and recognize opportunities are strong plusses. The best mentors are able to discern what makes their mentees tick, are not afraid to try things the latter consider fun or interesting, and are even open to be transformed by the relationship. Happily, mentoring is a two-way street: the process is a chance for each party to grow and learn, with a good number of mentors reporting that what they get out of the relationship is just as significant as what their respective mentees receive. For many boomers, mentoring has served as a vehicle to grow as people and gain greater insight into their own inner self. Being a mentor also often heightens one's self-confidence, contributes to the feeling they are changing the world a little bit for the better, and leads to a more acute perception of racial or ethnic difference. Finally, mentoring typically makes one like one's job more, improves one's family life, and, last but not least, is an opportunity to have a lot of fun. Before being assigned a mentee, candidates are of course trained, and, throughout the mentoring relationship, receive ongoing education and support. Boomers who feel ready can use the Mentoring Connector on mentoring.org—the only national mentoring database.[13]

OPPORTUNITY

Support MENTOR's efforts to help boomers pay it forward.

TEACHING

Like many predictions about baby boomers, the one about hordes of them retiring as soon as they reached age 65 has not materialized. This holds true for many professions but especially for teaching, a field that many boomers entered in droves after graduating from college in the 1970s and 1980s. Boomers' hesitation about leaving their teaching gigs has turned out to be a good thing, as millennials have shown a remarkable disinterest in taking their jobs. In California, for example, 55 percent fewer people enrolled in teacher training courses in 2012 than did in 2008, the California Commission on Teacher Credentialing reported. A 2016 nationwide study of college freshmen, meanwhile, revealed that there would likely be fewer education majors in this country in more than four decades. Only 4 percent of those surveyed planned to declare education as their major—the usual initial sign one intends to become a teacher—versus 11 percent back in 1971, according to UCLA's Cooperative Institutional Research Program. Not only are fewer American students interested in teaching, but many mid-career teachers in their thirties and forties are leaving for less stressful, better paid jobs, making some think that a real crisis in education is heading our way.[14]

Fortunately, more boomers wanting to pay it forward are entering the teaching profession as an encore career. Before checking out of their original career, some are attending courses at community colleges and in certified programs to parlay their career experience into teaching. After receiving teaching credentials, these 50- and 60-somethings are finding paying jobs, often in No Child Left Behind core academic subjects such as math and science as well as special education. Besides viewing it as an opportunity to pass on one's knowledge, teaching offers boomers the chance to take on a challenge, stay active, and supplement their savings—all good reasons why a fair number are heading to classrooms. Because of the dire need for qualified teachers across the country, all 50 states allow those interested in becoming one to substitute professional experience for a degree in education in order to fast track the process. As Chapter 3 mentioned, some companies help pay for employees to become encore career teachers. IBM's "Transition to Teaching" program, for example, grants up to $15,000 to employees with 10 years or greater tenure at the company who are interested in entering the educational arena, something for which they are often well suited. With math and science teachers in particular demand, ex-IBMers often find they can apply their knowledge in a new way, a win-win situation for all.[15]

Why are boomers interested in becoming teachers when they could be doing many other things after ending their original careers? Almost all of us are able to remember a particular teacher who was truly inspirational or even changed our life in some way—the essence of paying it forward. Teaching also is essential to shaping the next generation, another expression of Erikson's concept of "generativity." It's an overused expression, but teaching is "the toughest job you'll ever love," the only real way to explain why people would take on such a tough and demanding challenge in their third act of life. Because they have a few decades of work experience, often in corporate settings, boomers are helping to bring a much-needed sense of professionalism to education. In part because of older adults entering the field, education in America is again gradually gaining the respect it deserves, something that will pay off big dividends down the road as global competition accelerates.[16]

While there are no precise numbers for how many boomers are becoming first-time teachers, a survey by the National Center for Education Information found that about a third of new hires were "delayed entrants," that is, people who did not enter the field immediately after college. A prime site for boomers interested in teaching is teach.org, a unique collaboration between Microsoft and the U.S. Department of Education and endorsed by the country's leading educational and teaching organizations. The federal government had not been able to launch and manage a nationwide employment database allowing individuals to locate teaching opportunities, but that changed with Microsoft's participation. As well, the company came up with an easy way for potential teachers to determine how to progress from taking courses in the field all the way to getting certified, something that has been a Byzantine process.[17]

Microsoft's involvement in teach.org is a reflection of the company's decades long, global commitment to education. Much in part to Microsoft cofounder Bill Gates's personal philosophy, the company maintains that all children warrant a first-rate education and is thus doing what it can to further that wonderful endeavor. The company has a solid relationship with the global education community to make possible, as Microsoft states, "improved learning outcomes for all." "Ensuring access to high quality teachers for all students in the United States is essential to fulfilling this mission," it adds, explaining Microsoft's unprecedented level of commitment to the field of education and our collective future.[18]

KNOWLEDGE TRANSFER

Although the anticipated mass exit of baby boomers from the workplace has yet to take place, many executives are deeply worried about the expertise that will disappear from their companies when it eventually does happen. After being at their jobs for decades, boomers will leave a vacuum of intellectual capital should they decide to quit, the thinking goes, causing major problems that will take years from which to recover. Out of this concern has sprung the idea of "knowledge transfer"—the passing on of boomers' perspective, insight, and skill sets to a generation of younger employees.[19]

Importantly, knowledge transfer includes not just the steps required to complete a particular task—how to run a meeting or how to write a document, say—but how to think about and solve problems. Maintaining and building relationships with those on the outside is also part of the equation, as is how to best present the organization to the business community and general public. It ain't the first rodeo for boomer employees, one might say, their having seen a similar issue or challenge many times before of great value in tackling a new one.[20] In short, experience is a key asset for any organization, something more high-level managers are realizing as they look at their older employees and wonder when they will decide to call it a career.

Some boomers are already ending their first careers, the impetus for companies to figure out how to best transfer boomers' knowledge to Gen Xers and millennials. Just as they reshaped culture, music, fashion, politics, and the economy, boomers are reinventing the workplace through their gradual exit. Four million boomers a year are believed to be leaving the workforce, more than half in leadership posts. "What's lost is a wealth of accumulated skills and experience, relationships and networks cultivated over years, and firsthand recollections about the development of products, services, and marketing strategies," wrote Eric F. Frazier for business.com in 2015. Employees in most organizations have experienced a scare when they realize the only person who knows how to get a certain thing done, reach a specific contact, or locate a needed document has, like Elvis, left the building.[21]

Generational dynamics are playing a key role in of transfer of boomers' workplace knowledge. While boomers and Gen Xers tend to communicate effectively, the former and millennials are apt to think and act differently, a challenge for employers. (Millennials are in fact now the largest generation in the U.S. labor force, with one in three workers part of this 53.5 million-strong cohort.) For example, boomers like to meet in person and deliver information verbally—often for extended periods of time, much to the chagrin of millennials. Most younger folks do not like long meetings and would actually prefer to work at home using online tools, a difference in generational styles that can make the transfer of knowledge a tricky process. According to the U.S. Bureau of Labor Statistics, boomer-heavy jobs include business analysis, engineering, finance, union work, postal work, law enforcement, nursing, social work, and law, making it those occupations in which there is likely to be a knowledge gap.[22]

As companies both large and small embrace the idea of knowledge transfer, documenting how boomers do their jobs before they depart has become recognized as crucial to avoid a "brain drain." Much of this knowledge is experiential rather than written down, meaning it's not as simple as handing over a file folder. Losing technical knowledge is a particular concern for organizations whose senior engineers are planning to bow out. What is in boomers' heads can't be simply replaced by a new hire, as literally no one is likely to have the "deep smarts" of a person who held a particular job since the Reagan administration. Making the situation even more problematic is millennials' habit of changing jobs every few years, as they take their newly inherited knowledge with them when they walk out the door.[23] (To be fair, boomers also job hopped like rabbits when they were in their twenties when they saw a bigger opportunity knocking at the door.)

A variety of steps are being taken to allow boomers to pay their knowledge forward to younger employees. Some companies are creating diverse, intergenerational project teams, while others are putting boomers and millennials together in social settings outside the office to try to build workplace relationships. Job rotation exposes younger people to different parts of a business before they specialize in one particular area, and "job shadowing," where apprentices follow boomers around for a few months, has become another way to transfer knowledge. Many companies take videos of boomers explaining a certain business process, a useful tool for more methodical tasks. General Motors is doing as much as any company to retain institutional knowledge but finds itself increasingly hiring older ex-employees as consultants, a smart way to extend and spread their expertise.[24] Boomers are directly responsible for one of the most successful business and production periods in American history, so companies should be doing whatever they can to help the generation achieve one last great achievement: bestow their knowledge for future generations.

OPPORTUNITY

Reinvest boomers' intellectual capital in younger workers.

COACHING

A good number of boomers who do leave their full-time jobs find that coaching is an ideal next career. With extensive life and, often, business experience, boomers are ideal candidates to become coaches, whether in a professional or personal capacity. Coaches show clients how to best apply their talents in a meaningful way, sometimes requiring the latter to make major life changes. (The International Coach Federation considers coaching to be "partnering with clients in a thought-provoking and creative process that inspires them to maximize their personal and professional potential.") According to the Hay Group, 25–40 percent of Fortune 500 companies hire executive (or professional, corporate, and business) coaches, with boomers serving as most of those consultants. Coaching is an opportunity to capitalize on one's experience by giving back to others and make very decent money in the process. Successful life coaches typically earn more than $75,000 a year and experienced executive coaches well over $100,000 a year—a lot more than what one's income from Social Security is likely to be.[25]

Being in the business, companies that train people to be coaches recognize that boomers are well suited to the profession. "With [boomers'] vast business and life experience and the desire to help others succeed and have more fulfilling lives and careers, they are simply too young to retire," states the Institute for Professional Excellence in Coaching (iPEC) on its website, adding that coaching "is calling to them because it is one of the few professions that fully capitalizes on their experience, values, and 'pay it forward' attitude." Research conducted by the International Coach Federation and PriceWaterhouseCoopers in 2012 found that almost 40 percent of coaches in the United States, Canada, and Mexico are 55 years old or more, with the number likely to increase as more baby boomers embark on encore careers. In a typical life coaching session, Luke Iorio, president and CEO of iPEC explains, a coach asks a lot of questions to challenge their client as a means of encouraging him or her to forge an implementable plan. "Life coaching is meant to propel forward action, showing clients how to increase their self-awareness, clarify their goals, raise their confidence and commitment and identify paths," Iorio says, things virtually everyone could benefit from.[26]

Because the ideal executive coach is likely to have had his or her professional dreams come true, he or she is the right person to enable others to achieve that worthy goal. Over the course of decades of business experience almost always culminating in a leadership role, 60-something executive coaches have faced the struggles of corporate life and went through the ups and downs that come with every career. That experience helps younger managers to navigate their own professional journey, making executive coaches well worth the investment for companies grooming future leaders. Before they became coaches, most boomers were already those kind of people to whom others came for advice and, more often than not, had good ideas for solving problems. Coaches take great pleasure in seeing others grow and are inclined to take action when seeing that people are not taking advantage of their full potential. Like therapists, coaches recognize they have a certain gift for helping others live a more fulfilling life, a wonderful thing to do after completing one's own career goals.[27]

In her 2015 article "Why Baby Boomers Make Great Executive Coaches" for LinkedIn, Kimberli Lewis cites reasons such as boomers' high work ethic, their desire to "do better than their parents," and their wish to contribute for why many are choosing coaching as an encore career. Whether having spent a quarter century in management or in service professions like health, law, and social services, boomers feel they can still make a difference, with coaching a logical choice. Besides the good money to be made, coaching also can offer flexibility, as one is able to work for oneself and Skype and FaceTime are commonly used. Business experience alone will not make one a good executive coach, however, and the field demands different skills than those of mentoring or consulting. Rather than just give advice based on experience, coaching "helps individuals find their own solutions and increase their performance through their own realizations," as Lewis, general manager of the Search & Information Industry Association, put it, not an easy thing to do. Happily, while millennials may not enjoy being lectured to by boomers for hours on end, they do enjoy having a coach, as it is somewhat of a status symbol within a company.[28]

Andrew Neitlich of the Center for Executive Coaching goes even further than Lewis in connecting boomers with coaching. For Neitlich, founder and director of that organization located near Sarasota, Florida, executive coaching is "a perfect career for recent retirees and baby boomers." Neitlich gets a lot of calls from SCORE volunteers who are interested in becoming executive coaches. SCORE (the Service Corps of Retired Executives) offers gratis business advice to entrepreneurial types, a wonderful thing in itself. But with the chance to earn a great income while still working from home and making one's own hours, it's not surprising that SCORE volunteers want to pass on their experience and lessons learned through executive coaching.[29]

OPPORTUNITY

Count on more boomers paying it forward through coaching.

ADOPTING

For some baby boomers, paying it forward means investing in a deeper, more personal experience than volunteering, mentoring, teaching, coaching, or passing on their knowledge to younger employees. Although well into their fifties or even sixties, more boomers are adopting children, disproving the belief that there is a certain cut-off point to be a good parent. Again, there are few numbers to know how many boomers are adopting kids because no organization or federal agency keeps track, but "without question," says Adam Pertman, author of *Adoption Nation*, "more of them are doing it." (Celebrity boomer adopters include Diane Keaton, who adopted a daughter in 1996 at age 50 and a son in 2001 at age 55; Sharon Stone adopted a child at age 48 in 2006, and Sheryl Crow was 49 when she adopted a son in 2001.) Some boomer adopters are women who had busy careers and never got around to getting married and having children but now have the time and determination to do so. Others had fertility problems and finally decided to adopt, while yet others had a child who had died at an early age. Women who have become widows have been known to adopt a child, seeing it as an opportunity to start a new family. Grandparents who are taking care of grandchildren because their parents are unable to for some reason is a whole other matter, but one that is unfortunately taking place more frequently.[30]

Increased life spans have something to do with boomers choosing to adopt a child. With average life expectancy now about 80, a 50-year-old could adopt a child and live long enough to have grandkids, quite an amazing thing. Another positive is that boomers often prefer to adopt an older child—something most younger adults prefer not to do. (Some boomer adoptees are just months away from being aged out of the foster care system.)[31] Over 100,000 American children under 18 are waiting to be adopted, with more than half of those over the age of 6, making older parents more and more welcome by social workers. Over the last couple of decades, age parameters set by adoption groups have broadened, allowing more qualified older adults to become parents. (Adoption candidates have to pass a rigorous background check and take part in a home study process in which a case worker observes the family before getting the go-ahead.)[32] Boomer adoption is thus good for society on a number of levels and a way for older parents to make one more, lasting contribution.

A high percentage of boomer adopters have grown children who sometimes have children themselves. As Chapter 6 discussed, new grandparents can find themselves parenting, something mom and dad are usually not too keen on. Such grandparents can conclude they're not done parenting, impetus for them to explore adoption. Boomers' kids as well as their friends are apt to think this 50- or 60-something couple has, in short, gone nuts when they hear the exciting news. But all tend to come around when they see the couple's parenting skills, which perhaps can be best described as "don't sweat the small stuff." Boomer parents are likely to be more patient than younger ones, a result of their life experience and ability to keep things in perspective. (Greater financial stability is another big plus.) Those who never had children but do in their third act of life often feel a great sense of gratitude, having realized something they likely believed never would happen. Boomers who had idyllic childhoods are more inclined to become adopters, as they see parenting as a gift they can bestow on those in a less fortunate position. A fair share of boomers adopters go to another country (China, Cambodia, Ethiopia, Belarus, Bulgaria, and the Ukraine are among the more popular) to find their child.[33]

Two major life events—ending one's original career and becoming an empty nester—can trigger a boomer's desire to adopt a child. What greater purpose in life is there to raise a child? boomers who experienced one or both of these events ask themselves. Given the alternatives—socializing, relaxing, or working on one's bucket list, say—adopting a child in one's third act of life does take considerable fortitude. But does age matter when it comes to parenting? Curiously, not much. The incredible variety of families these days makes being an older (or single, gay, or disabled) mom or dad not that odd.[34] (I had my first and only child at age 55 and, except for occasionally being mistaken for a granddad rather than a dad, it's pretty much business as usual.) Energy can be an issue (following my 5-year-old around ain't easy, trust me), but the joy of being an older parent makes up for the feeling of being wiped out at the end of a play-filled day. In fact, many boomers report that adopting a child helps keep them young, if not physically then psychologically. After all, boomer parents go through the same kind of things that younger people do, such as ferrying children around to birthday parties or experiencing the holidays in a way that only a kid can. "Adoption isn't always easy, but sometimes there is a child out there just waiting to belong to you," said one woman who adopted a son at age 50, adding that "it doesn't matter how old you are, it just matters that you've got love to give."[35]

OPPORTUNITY

Support adoption as more boomers pursue the definitive form of paying it forward.

TEN

Footprints in the Sand

The measure of a person's life is the affect they have on others.
Ex-professional basketball player Steve Nash

What's a good way for an older person to become less depressed, have lower blood pressure, and live longer? Give money and/or time to a cause in which he or she believes. Many studies show that giving and volunteering are good for one's health, as being generous is an important source of happiness for those who choose to do it. Older givers are not just happier and healthier than non-givers but also have a stronger sense of purpose and higher self-esteem, more reason to be excited about the philanthropic windfall that is looming as baby boomers age. It turns out that helping people in need offers a greater opportunity to be find joy in life than spending money on oneself, something that perhaps should make all of us question our priorities.

This final chapter of *Boomers 3.0*, Footprints in the Sand, recognizes the increasing value of leaving something behind after one is gone. Creating some form of legacy is top of mind for many boomers, as more and more ask themselves, "How can or will I be remembered?" It is difficult to overestimate boomers' interest in making others know that they spent some time on Earth, in the process realizing a legitimate form of immortality. Need it be said, this is a highly valuable pursuit and a genuine way to effectively extend one's lifespan or live forever (versus the false promise of antiaging). Older people have historically been the biggest givers because they are more likely to have the resources to do so and due to their natural inclination to help pave the way for the next generation. (Upward of 90% of Americans aged 65 or older give in some way.) This will hold true for boomers as they age, making many nonprofit causes giddy with excitement because of their numbers. Boomers already contribute about 43 percent of all dollars given in the United States, a study by the software firm Blackbaud found, the highest percentage of any generation to date.[1]

Boomers have two primary ways to leave their footprints in the sand: money and time. Boomers are expected to donate $8 trillion to charities over the following 20 years in either money or time as volunteers, according to a 2015 study conducted by Merrill Lynch, a transfer of wealth that will reshape the philanthropic landscape of the country and world. "Boomers are famous for wanting to do things their own way and change the world, and charitable giving will be the next chapter in their impact," wrote Allison Pond in the *Deseret News*, with most "wanting to be more personally involved in the causes they care about."[2] Making real, measurable change is the goal, replacing the previous model of charity in which complete trust was placed with nonprofits to spend money as they saw fit. Boomers tend to "invest" in a charity rather than just give it away, seeing their contribution as "philanthropic venture capital." More than anything else, boomer philanthropy will be driven by individual passions—the very same way they have spent their money since they had any to spend. Invite boomers to leave their footprints in the sand, my final recommendation goes, by creating relevant foundations, trusts, philanthropies, and nonprofits and by offering innovate ways to volunteer their time.

OPPORTUNITY

Pitch boomers the ultimate pitch—a legacy.

BOOMER PHILANTHROPY

Blackbaud's report on giving has only reinforced charities' fund-raising efforts directed to baby boomers. Boomers are more generous than any other age group both in terms of number of donors and percentage of all donations. Boomers currently account for 43 percent of the $143.6 billion in estimated annual contributions, while Matures give 26 percent, Gen Xers 20 percent, and Gen Yers (millennials) 11 percent. Boomers are increasingly giving online, much to fund-raisers' delight, something

Matures are very unlikely to do. Giving through Facebook, Twitter, and other social networks remains low, however, as is contributing money via text. Boomers are giving less money and volunteer time to religious organizations than their parents' generation but are still much more inclined to support religious groups than millennials and Generation Xers. Relatively few boomers are volunteering at animal-rights and environmental groups or giving money to human rights charities compared with millennials.[3]

While billion dollar gifts from the likes of Bill Gates and Warren Buffet make the headlines, it's millions of small donations—most of them by boomers—that made charitable giving hit a record high in 2015. More people give to charity than vote, a study by the Giving USA Foundation and the Indiana University Lilly Family School of Philanthropy found, with gifts of $20 or less adding up to hundreds of billions of dollars. Interestingly, while giving was up by 4 percent that year, money going to foundations was down by that same percentage, a slippage that likely reflects the large and impersonal nature of those charitable organizations. Charity going to religions has been a diminishing piece of the philanthropic pie for many years but it still represents the largest single category of donations. Religions received $119 billion in 2015, followed by education ($57 billion), human services ($45 billion), foundations ($42 billion), health ($30 billion), public benefit ($27 billion), arts ($17 billion), international ($16 billion), and environment ($11 billion).[4]

Although the pickins are already extremely good, many charities have so far had a difficult time clicking with boomers. One reason could be that boomers may be delaying their biggest giving because most of them are still working, and that they are planning the bulk of their philanthropic activities for their next chapter. As well, much has been made of boomers' lack of savings, so perhaps many of them are building up their respective nest eggs before fully devoting themselves to philanthropic efforts.[5] The most likely reason for some nonprofits' inability to crack the philanthropic code of boomers, however, is the latter's role as "professional" consumers. Highly educated and famously shrewd when it comes to marketing pitches, boomers are a tough sell for anything, especially for something as intangible as a cause. But the more education a person has, the more likely he or she will donate money, a general rule of philanthropy goes, something many charities are hanging their hats on. Boomers' commitment to volunteering also bodes well for the future of philanthropy. (Giving money and volunteering time to a particular cause often go together.) Boomers are currently at a 10-year high for nonprofit involvement, according to a recent Corporation for National and Community Service study, with approximately one-third of people over age 55 volunteering. That represents more than 20 million people giving three billion service hours, which equates to about $67 billion in monetary value—an astounding figure by any measure.[6]

Perhaps the biggest reason to be bullish on boomer philanthropy is their growing social conscience as they age. "More and more, as the baby boomers enter their final life stage, it looks like they're coming together— as they did in the 1960s—to solve the significant issues of our time," wrote Kn Moy of Masterworks, a consulting company serving Christian organizations, seeing their collective future as "bold and consequential." Boomers' interest in tackling the tough problems of the day is also personal; each one has an idea of how to make the world a better place for their kids and grandkids. This meshing of post-countercultural idealism and individualism is emerging as the guiding model of philanthropy. "Across each life stage, boomers rejected the status quo as they reinvented technology, culture, politics, and the entire social scene," Moy continued, "and they'll more than likely reinvent philanthropy."[7]

In the meantime, boomers are leaning toward local charities when donating money. According to the Blackbaud report, boomers prioritize places of worship (38%) and local social service organizations (36%) over all other types of charities, with children's charities (22%) coming in a distant third. Trade unions (0%) and election campaigns (2%) obviously rank low for boomers in terms of giving. What's the single most compelling reason for a boomer to choose one charity over another? Research suggests that an emotional appeal from a nonprofit backed up by a strong and positive reputation is the winning formula, although many other factors no doubt come into play in the decision—the most important being personal relevance.[8]

OPPORTUNITY

Win boomer loyalty by building in philanthropic causes to your brands' deliverables.

DONOR-ADVISED FUNDS

With personal relevance the backbone to baby boomer giving, donor-advised funds (DAFs) are ideally positioned as a form of philanthropy.

As the name suggests, donors act as advisors of how their charitable organization or financial institution fund will be used by retaining privileges to make grant recommendations when and how they wish. Fidelity, Schwab, and Vanguard are the big three of the latter; each of those companies' charitable funds ranks among the nation's wealthiest 100 nonprofits alongside heavily endowed hospital networks and Ivy League universities. DAFs may be established with cash, securities, or other property, and, importantly, donations to the fund are immediately tax deductible when grant recommendations are made to a recognized 501(c) (3) public charity. Another plus of these increasingly popular accounts is that unspent funds continue to grow tax-free—a bone of contention among critics who view DAFs as a kind of tax shelter.[9]

For both financial and altruistic reasons, however, DAFs are flying through the roof as a way for boomers and others to leave footprints in the sand. (They are in fact the fastest-growing form of charity in the United States.) Contributing to donor-advised funds and grants given through them climbed to records in 2015, according to the latest 2016 Donor-Advised Fund Report produced by the National Philanthropic Trust (NPT). That report revealed that DAF grants to nonprofits grew 17 percent in 2015, from $12.42 billion to $14.52 billion. Contributions hit another historic peak of $22.26 billion, making up 8.4 percent of the $264.58 billion in charitable giving by Americans. Why the double-digit growth? The most numerous and most generous givers—boomers—wish to be closely connected to their philanthropic ventures and are interested in tracking their charitable impact, according to Eileen Heisman, CEO of the NPT. In addition, DAFs offer the opportunity to donate noncash assets, something that offers major tax advantages for those in upper-income brackets. Illiquid asset donations are in fact a rapidly filling philanthropic pool, ranging from "complex securities," private company stock, hedge fund assets, real estate holdings, and antique furniture and jewelry. (Even the cryptocurrency Bitcoin is considered to be an acceptable DAF contributing asset.) Gifting highly appreciated stocks allows donors to save on capital gains taxes that they would have otherwise incurred had they sold those securities and given the cash.[10]

Beyond their flexibility, tax advantages, and making possible the ability to be in control of one's own philanthropic mission, DAFs offer an opportunity to leave a unique family legacy. "How do we communicate our values to children and grandchildren?" asks Carol Wolf, managing director of planned giving and endowments at the Jewish Federation of Cleveland. DAFs can help start this discussion, she believes, recommending that all generations of a family be included in the process in order to demonstrate one's personal values and the importance of philanthropy in general. One can ask children to recommend grants of a certain amount each year, or gather at holiday dinners to make philanthropic choices together, she suggests, with DAFs serving as a wonderful catalyst for family philanthropy. Donor-advised accounts are often named as the "X Family Fund," this itself a way to carry a family's name forward.[11]

Fidelity Charitable has a keen understanding of the role that family can play in DAFs, a big part why they now rank as the top nonprofit fundraiser in the United States (and the second-largest donor to charities in the country, after the Bill & Melinda Gates Foundation). Fidelity even surpassed the mother of all charities—United Way—for the first time in 2015, as customers put $4.6 billion into the fund's gift accounts. The ability for clients to park charitable dollars without having to make an immediate decision about where to direct the money—not to mention the tax break—is obviously a big draw for investors. If Fidelity Charitable notices that a client has not made a donation from an account in three years, it suggests that a contribution be made; if an account is inactive for six years, Fidelity will make donations on that donor's behalf. The average Fidelity Charitable account holder is hardly a Thurston Howell III; the average account size is $15,000, with boomers donating about $2,000 a year.[12]

Again, much of Fidelity's phenomenal success with DAFs has to do with what it calls "the power of family giving." Philanthropy among relatives often brings together families over time and through space, serving as a kind of bridge, the company explains to potential investors. Incorporating philanthropy into the lives of younger family members is an opportunity to send a positive message about money and the importance of serving those in need. Fidelity recommends families take five steps to manage a giving program: (1) have family members articulate their giving goals; (2) develop a family mission statement; (3) decide where to give; (4) select a giving vehicle; and (5) assess the impact. "Philanthropy can strengthen family ties by offering family members a unique opportunity to articulate and act on their shared values," agrees Betsy Brill, president of Chicago-based Strategic Philanthropy, Ltd., seeing DAFs in particular as "an effective means of passing on your family's philanthropic legacy through the generations."[13]

OPPORTUNITY

Help boomers pass on their philanthropic legacy through the generations.

ENDOWMENTS

As with donor-advised funds, baby boomers are using endowments as a means to, in a sense, live forever. An endowment is "a financial asset, in the form of a donation made to a non-profit group, institution or individual consisting of investment funds or other property that may or may not have a stated purpose at the bequest of the donor," according to investopedia. com. The philanthropic motherlode is yet to come, but a fair number of boomers are currently establishing endowments (sometimes referred to as "forever gifts") in order to see some of the fruits of their labor. "Seeking immediate gratification and a desire to witness the results of their largesse, some boomers prefer to launch endowments now," wrote Jackie Jacobs, CEO of the Columbus Jewish Foundation, while "others arrange to establish endowments later on with estate assets." Some plan to do both by starting an endowment now and adding more over time or through a bequest provision.[14]

Why are many boomers specifically interested in endowments as a form of legacy? It is not difficult to find a cause that mirrors one's particular passions and values, something entirely in sync with boomers' desire to personalize their philanthropy. "Attaching their names to such funds gives them an enduring legacy that immortalizes their optimism," Jacobs explained, thinking "the ability to influence succeeding generations and remind others of their values has great appeal."[15] Clearly, it is the perpetuity of an endowment fund that is its most attractive feature, as it is difficult to imagine anything more compelling than one's ideals continuing to be expressed through time. Endowments can be seen as a tangible expression of the same kind of commitment to social justice that boomers have had for the past half century. They may have had just a few bucks in the pockets of their torn Levis in the late 1960s, but today they likely have many more, some of which can be used to help achieve their lofty dreams.

Like DAFs, typical endowments are not the stuff of billionaires, making them within the reach of many givers. An endowment fund of $25,000 generating an annual revenue stream of $1,000 is not unusual and, like the Energizer Rabbit, it keeps on going. Precisely because of that, many nonprofits across the country are pushing to raise endowments, a tough assignment but well worth the effort given the possibility of having a reliable and sustainable source of revenue.[16] Boomers' interest in endowments is thus very good news to nonprofits. "Donors, especially baby boomers, are increasingly looking to contribute to endowments to ensure their gifts have a lasting legacy," Sherri Welch of *Crain's Detroit*

Business noted, a much different story than in the past when donors would typically make an outright gift to a nonprofit and allow its board to decide how it should be used per the organization's mission. But designating a gift for an endowed fund and restricting its purpose is the best opportunity to have a long-term impact, many donors feel, resulting in a kind of philanthropy many nonprofits have never seen before. It was not unheard of for organizations to turn down such demands in the past but, now that they are becoming business as usual, defined endowments are actually the gift of choice.[17]

As endowments become more popular, not just larger institutions like health systems and universities but smaller ones are trying to get in on the action. Arts and culture organizations in particular recognize the value of endowments. In the Detroit area, for example, the Detroit Institute of Arts, the Detroit Symphony Orchestra, and the Arab American National Museum are planning or in the midst of renewed campaigns to raise endowment funds. "It's a bank of money we know will be there," said the director of that museum of endowments, seeing them as a source of "unrestricted funds which provide a certain level of freedom and, in many ways, it's guaranteed." Even local libraries and churches are unveiling endowment campaigns as a buffer against the kind of economic downturn we had in 2008.[18]

Also eyeing boomers as a source of "forever funding" through endowments is the U.S. National Park Service. Established a century ago, the national parks were intended to be preserved for as long as the country was around, but keeping them going is obviously an expensive proposition. Since they were tots being driven around in the back of station wagons, boomers have had a close relationship with the national parks, something that the service is hoping will result in generous gift giving as they age. According to a recent study sponsored by the National Park Foundation, a whopping 95 percent of households surveyed believe in the importance of protecting national parks for current and future generations. The national parks currently do not have an endowment, however, something that both environmentalists and some members of Congress feel has to change if they are to continue to survive for the next century. "Such an endowment would be an attractive vehicle for philanthropy especially now that the baby boomer generation is in the midst of transferring the largest amount of wealth in American history," wrote Julie Seger on the National Park Foundation blog, a worthy endeavor indeed.[19]

OPPORTUNITY

Create innovative endowment opportunities to capture boomers' "forever funding."

FAMILY FOUNDATIONS

For those baby boomers of some means who want even greater control over their giving and fewer restrictions than DAFs and endowments can offer, a nonprofit family foundation may be the way to go. A family foundation is a nonprofit, grant-making entity in which financial assets come from immediate family members.[20] One or more family members have to be donors and act as officers or be on the board of the foundation. Family foundations have increased greatly in number over the last decade or two, with more than 40,000 in the United States today making grants of over $20 billion a year. (There were just 3,200 such entities giving away almost $7 billion in 2001, according to the Foundation Center.) Family foundations are now hitting critical mass as boomers cash out from their jobs. "Family foundations are quickly springing up across the country as baby boomers sell successful businesses or take buyouts from top corporate jobs," noted Kelly Greene of the *Wall Street Journal* in explaining the phenomenon.[21]

Why are family foundations becoming increasingly popular among boomers who have more money than they need? Like DAFs and endowments, there are tax breaks to be had, of course, but family foundations allow philanthropists more ability to call the shots than other charitable vehicles. And because they are literally family operations, such foundations offer an even greater possibility of teaching the importance of social responsibility to children and grandchildren. "There is often an underlying desire for baby boomers to instill in their children the significance of giving and compassion for those less privileged," observed Kerry Hannon of the *New York Times*, thinking "a family foundation can curb a sense of entitlement that may come along with inheriting wealth."[22]

Not everyone creating a family foundation is a gazillionaire, however. Sixty percent of such foundations hold assets of below a million bucks, in fact, with those forming them most interested in having a significant but specific impact with what is often a relatively small amount of money. Billionaires like Steve Case and Bill Gates may be trying to eradicate major diseases with their foundations (such large-scale efforts are often labeled "strategic philanthropy"), but average Joes who have done pretty well for themselves have much more modest ambitions. Family foundations can offer the biggest bang for the buck by encouraging direct participation in philanthropy, something most other charitable avenues do not allow. Instilling the value of giving back among younger generations is an essential part of family foundations, with leaving a legacy a tangible way to measure the transition from "success to significance" that Kadlec and Dychwald talked about in their book. Adult children often sit on the board of family foundations, a commitment of time that pays off when they become the principal donors. By law, family foundations have to annually donate about 5 percent of assets or else be hit with a 30 percent excise tax on that part which hasn't been doled out, as well as annually file IRS Form 990. (The IRS searches for clues that a member of the family is treating the foundation as his or her own piggy bank—an accusation with which the president of the United States has some familiarity.)[23]

Perhaps the best thing about family foundations is their ability to unite family members with a common purpose. Determining who should be the recipient of funds is a way to share a mutual mission—something most families cannot say they possess. One family starting a foundation visited rural villages in Africa to see how their money could be used, for example, a literally once-in-a-lifetime-experience that helped bring family members closer together. All families occasionally squabble, however, especially when money is involved, making foundations a potential source of conflict. Younger members of a family may also hesitate getting involved should they not relate to the cause(s) the foundation is supporting. Feeling smothered by bossy parents or simply not having the time or abilities to manage a foundation are other reasons for children to pass.[24]

To that end, experts suggest five steps family foundations should take to get kids interested in carrying on a legacy of charitable work:

1. Tell the story: Provide the reasons why the foundation was begun in order to encourage young people to get involved;

2. Train them early: Exposing kids to charitable giving is an ideal way to have them more fully commit when they are adults;

3. Give them a voice and a vote: Without a voice and a vote, younger family members may lose interest in the family's philanthropic work;

4. Be open to change: Older family members need to be open to fresh ideas so younger heirs can carry on the family's philanthropic legacy; and

5. Give them time: Becoming a philanthropist is an "evolution" that often takes time, so it's important not to pressure younger family members into taking on big foundation roles before they are ready. Foundations should provide enough flexibility to allow younger family members to stay involved with whatever level of commitment they're capable of giving.[25]

OPPORTUNITY

Show boomers how they can create their own family's philanthropic legacy.

ESG INVESTING

Yet another way that baby boomers are making a positive, lasting impact is Environmental, Social and Governance (ESG) investing. Choosing to invest in companies that have a positive social impact and avoiding those that have a negative one, like major polluters or those that have poor corporate governance structures, is quite literally putting one's money where one's mouth is. ESG (or "mission-driven") investment entails financial support of nonprofit organizations, companies that are socially responsible, and businesses managed by entrepreneurs with a social conscience. A growing number of boomers want their investments to match their values, sparking the growth of socially screened mutual funds. Rather than just one-offs, ESG investing is being increasingly packaged into funds like the Bay Area Equity Fund managed by JP Morgan, which strives to realize average yields while at the same time creating employment opportunities in lower-income areas.[26]

ESG investments exemplify the transition from "socially responsible investing" (SRI), which has long been an attractive option for those not wanting to support "bad" corporations based on certain criteria. SRI usually excluded "sin industries" like tobacco, alcohol, gambling, military hardware, as well as environmentally insensitive companies. ESG, on the other hand, prioritizes selectivity over avoidance in portfolio design. Rather than eliminating certain industries or companies, ESG investing is based on choosing organizations that consistently enforce corporate governance, are environmentally friendly, or confront significant social issues. Corporate governance involves being transparent, disclosing any potential conflicts or misconduct, keeping investors informed, and incentivizing positive change. Environmental friendliness encompasses minimal usage of natural resources, a reliance on alternative forms of energy and "clean" technologies, and an acknowledgment that global warming is real. Examples of addressing social issues are creating safer work environments, treating people of color fairly, and having a progressive stance toward females.[27]

While not philanthropy per se, ESG investing is a way to use one's money to benefit society, explaining its sharp rise over the past few years. Fifty-one percent of boomers surveyed in a recent Nielsen survey are willing to sacrifice some financial returns for sustainable offerings, in fact, showing how strongly the group feels about it. ESG investments grew 76 percent between 2012 and 2014 in the United States, from $3.74 trillion to $6.57 trillion. There are now more than 100 "sustainable" mutual funds in the country, offering investors a wider range of stocks and bonds from which to choose. Investors are particularly interested in companies that have reduced carbon footprints, reflecting the growing concern over climate change, that is, global warming. Companies that use less energy and emit less waste are also at least in theory more efficient, something that should help improve their bottom line.[28] Not just boomers but millennials are keen on supporting socially responsible companies, making ESG investing something that is helping to bridge the generations. "The multigenerational, broad-based appeal of values-based investing, along with an increased focus on sustainability and other social issues within the U.S., makes it easy to understand why demand for these types of investments has skyrocketed in the last 10 years," Scott Stanley of Pharos Wealth Management wrote for LinkedIn in 2016.[29]

Investment managers are stepping up by incorporating more refined screening criteria to identify such companies for their portfolio strategies. Three sets of ESG-consistent criteria are typically considered: corporate governance (an organization's top executives, how they are paid, self-regulation policies, and treatment of shareholders), environmental (the degree to which an organization acts as a protector of nature), and social (how an organization manages relationships with its employees). Several firms, including Sustainalytics, IW Financial, Thomson Reuters, MSCI and Morningstar, specialize in performing the kind of in-depth research necessary to evaluate the relative "ethicalness" of a given company.[30] The jury is still out whether socially responsible companies perform as well as others from a financial standpoint, but most experts agree that there is not much of a statistical difference. Opting for an ethical portfolio is thus a no-brainer, many feel, this itself encouraging more companies to be good citizens in order to attract investors.

Happily, more investors, portfolio advisors, and financial companies are signing the Principles for Responsible Investment (PRI), the loudest champion for investing responsibly. The PRI is endorsed by the United Nations but operates independently in promoting ESG principles, all the while making the case that investors who do so will do better financially in the long run. "We believe that an economically efficient, sustainable global financial system is a necessity for long-term value creation," goes PRI's mission, proposing that "such a system will reward long-term, responsible investment and benefit the environment and society as a whole."[31] ESG is not just the wave of the future but of the present, offering boomers the opportunity to leave their footprints in the sand.

OPPORTUNITY

Make sure your company is aligned with ESG principles to appeal to boomer investors.

CREATE THE GOOD

The name says it all. AARP's Create the Good program gets baby boomers together with others through volunteering, making it an opportunity for people to connect at a local level and, in the process, spread positive vibes across the country and around the world. Philanthropic investing is great but giving one's time is perhaps a more valuable and generous contribution as it is a finite resource. So far, 200,000 people have joined the Create the Good movement, each one somehow leaving his or her footprints in the sand. "Together we can make a difference," AARP tells potential volunteers, expressing the truism that "it only takes one person to help change the world." Much like VolunteerMatch and MENTOR, Create the Good is a matchmaking service that leverages the connectivity of the Internet. Volunteers sign up and are sent descriptions of gigs that are aligned with their experience and passions and learn of opportunities as soon as they are posted. Organizations, meanwhile, register to land qualified volunteers to be a part of their initiatives, all of this with no cost to anyone. Creating the good can mean providing food to the hungry, gathering resources for use in a classroom, establishing a communal gardening site, or hundreds of other positive experiences.[32]

Create the Good is steeped in AARP's core concept that everyone has some good to do. "The challenge is to live up to our better selves, to believe well of our fellow men and perhaps by doing so to help create the good, to experiment, to explore, to change, and to grow," said Ethel Percy Andrus, who founded AARP in 1958 (when she was 73).

Volunteerism runs through all levels of the organization: a voluntary Board of Directors and National Policy Council serves as leadership, with each of the its 53 statewide offices (including the District of Columbia, Puerto Rico, and the Virgin Islands) receiving leadership and guidance from a voluntary Executive Council along with another group of volunteers. Facilitating volunteerism is not surprisingly a key initiative of AARP. Many people, especially boomers, want flexibility to be embedded into volunteer opportunities, as they often have busy schedules and are interested in a wide range of pursuits. Create the Good is a testament to Dr. Andrus' primary ambition to serve others and goes beyond standard volunteering via its focus on meaningful connections, user-friendliness, and diverse set of opportunities.[33]

Many boomers looking to create the good on a larger canvas are using AARP to contribute globally. As Chapter 5 showed, combining travelling with volunteering is an ideal means of gaining exposure to different ways of life while also making a difference somewhere in the world. Should one choose volunteering while on a scheduled trip or travels with that expressed purpose, serving as a volunteer globally is a way to visit new, often off-the-beaten-track places, while also helping people. AARP's Office of International Affairs is an ideal resource for boomers wanting to leave their footprints somewhere in the world. That part of AARP acts as a kind of global diplomat or emissary by working with both governmental and nongovernmental organizations, corporations, and scholars to encourage an exchange of ideas on health care, economics, and other important subjects.[34]

Global volunteering is not necessarily a brief, one-off endeavor. A number of other globally oriented organizations present opportunities to volunteer for extended or recurring amounts of time, allowing travelers a greater chance to become immersed in a particular locale. HelpAge International, for example, works on behalf of older adults on a global basis by helping the poor, combatting ageism, and supporting other worthwhile causes. With a presence in more than 65 nations, HelpAge partners with a group of almost 300 organizations, leading to many inspirational enterprises likely to match one's interest and time commitment. HelpAge USA is part of that organization's worldwide entity assigned the task of carrying out initiatives designed to help older individuals who are living in poverty. Ensuring that such persons can receive assistance in emergencies, greater financial peace of mind, improved health care, and fairer treatment in general is a primary goal. HelpAge's vision is "a world in which all older people fulfill their potential to lead dignified, active, healthy, and secure lives," a cause to which boomers can likely relate. HelpAge is grounded in the basic tenet that older people possess the knowledge and determination to improve their lives and those of their families.[35]

Finally, the Peace Corps, probably the best-known organization to partner with volunteers, prepares and then stations people in more than 60 nations for a two-year stint. Such volunteer workers serve in a myriad of ways, ranging from teaching to farming and helping start a business. Shorter-term stays are also available for those not able to commit to two years. The Peace Corps makes available these less time-intensive assignments for those who have previously served in the organization, to those who have been employed at least 10 years, to people in the medical field, and to graduate students.[36] One more organization, the United Nations Volunteers, also makes possible opportunities for footprint leavers interested in a more just and peaceful world—as good a way as any to end the *Boomers 3.0* story.[37]

OPPORTUNITY

Create the good by helping boomers create the good.

Conclusion

Some years ago for a consulting project for J.P. Morgan, I spent considerable time venturing into the wilds of American wealth culture, documenting how rich people spent their time and money by using classic methods of cultural anthropology. In my "Wealthology" research, I found that there were five different psychological profiles or personality types of rich Americans, each kind comprising a subculture all its own. Not surprisingly, the study got quite a lot of attention (I was called "the Margaret Mead of plutocrats" by Slate.com), as Americans are notoriously fascinated with the lifestyles of the rich (and famous).

An expected and I believe even more interesting finding came out of the research, however. Over time and with more money, I learned, the American rich tended to evolve as human beings, becoming, in a sense, "better" people. Riffing on Maslow's hierarchy, I proposed that there is a kind of evolutionary ladder within American wealth culture, with those values associated with some millionaires falling "lower" on a scale of meaning and purpose than those of other millionaires. This important idea emerged out of my fieldwork indicating that most of the American rich were a "work in progress," trying to grow as human beings by swapping out personally defined interests and needs for those of others. Those folks who had found a "higher" purpose in their lives by somehow making the lives of other people better were infinitely happier and more secure (richer, so to speak) than those primarily interested in the acquisition of things or even experiences, I discovered, something that posed enormous implications for how we all might choose to live our lives.[1]

In my research for and during the writing process of this book, I found a remarkably similar yet equally unexpected thing: many baby boomers are going through an evolutionary process much like that of rich people, developing as human beings as they get older. As the following chart shows, there appears to be a kind of existential hierarchy within boomer culture grounded in the pursuit of meaning and purpose, as individuals strive for the next level along their unique journey of life.

BOOMER HIERARCHY

Pay It Forward; Footprints in the Sand	OTHER-DIRECTED
↑	
Boomerpods; Gray Power	GROUP-DIRECTED
↑	
Fountain of Youth; Old Dog, New Tricks; Reboot; Inner Muse; Bucket List; Higher Ground	SELF-DIRECTED

There are three levels within baby boomer culture, I suggest, with individuals moving "up" the hierarchy as they further evolve as human beings. The first six chapters of this book (Fountain of Youth; Old Dog, New Tricks; Reboot; Inner Muse; Bucket List; and Higher Ground) describe what I call self-directed behavior; the next two (Boomerpods and Gray Power) discuss what I call group-directed behavior; and the final two (Pay It Forward and Footprints in the Sand) examine what I call other-directed behavior. Self-directed behavior is generally me-oriented, meaning it revolves around the individual's wants or needs; group-directed behavior is generally communitarian in nature, meaning it involves multiple people having something in common; and other-directed behavior is dedicated to people other than the individual. This Boomer Hierarchy serves as an interesting model of baby boomers' life course, contending that people often "improve" as they age by moving away from self-oriented wants and needs to those of others.

Such a model not only adds deeper value to the content outlined in this book, but serves as additional fodder in terms of how to most effectively market to baby boomers in their third act of life. If indeed boomers are on a kind of journey in which they are moving toward group- or other-directed goals in order to find greater meaning and purpose in their lives, it would be in marketers' best interests to try to join them along that voyage. Marketers should ask themselves how their brands can be positioned as agents of altruism, and how they can help boomers reach a destination of wisdom or self-actualization. Enabling people to become more empathetic, wiser, and happier human beings is perhaps the ultimate unique selling proposition and one that smart marketers should embrace in order to take full advantage of this exciting time in American history.

Notes

INTRODUCTION

1. census.gov.
2. Val Srinivas and Urval Goradia, "The Future of Wealth in the United States," dupress.deloitte.com, November 9, 2015.
3. "Introducing Boomers: Marketing's Most Valuable Generation," nielsen.com, August 6, 2012.
4. Braden Phillips, "Marketers Take Second Look at Over-50 Consumers," nytimes.com, March 4, 2016.
5. Ibid.

CHAPTER 1. FOUNTAIN OF YOUTH

1. Lawrence R. Samuel, *Aging in America: A Cultural History* (University of Pennsylvania Press, 2017), 3.
2. Ibid., 3.
3. Ibid., 162.
4. Ibid., 149.
5. Ibid., 162–163.
6. Chelsea Kane, "How to Be an Optimum Ager: Keeping Your Brain in Shape as You Get Older," huffingtonpost.com, October 3, 2016.
7. Tara Parker-Pope, "Do Brain Workouts Work? Science Isn't Sure," nytimes.com, March 10, 2014.
8. lumosity.com.

9. happy-neuron.com.

10. cogmed.com.

11. neuronixmedical.com.

12. Constance Gustke, "For Effective Brain Fitness, Do More Than Play Simple Games," nytimes.com, July 8, 2016.

13. Ibid.

14. Tara Bahrampour, "Complex Jobs and Social Ties Appear to Help Ward Off Alzheimer's, New Research Shows," washingtonpost.com, July 25, 2016.

15. Lewis Richmond, "Is Meditation Buddhism Booming or Fading?," hufingtonpost.com, January 9, 2013.

16. Lynn Taylor Rick, "Boomers Take Advantage of Alternative Health Practices," rapidcityjournal.com, January 26, 2013.

17. Laura French, "The Art of Acupuncture," startribune.com, February 23, 2016.

18. Don Lee, "Preparing for the Coming Quake: Baby Boomer Demographics and TCM," acupuncturetoday.com, April 2012.

19. Jane Spencer, "Giving Up on Perfect Pecs, Boomers Embrace Qigong," wsj.com, May 13, 2003.

20. Ibid.

21. Pepper Schwartz, "Baby Boomers Getting Older but Not Giving Up on Sex," ashasexualhealth.org, August 1, 2014.

22. Ibid.

23. Alyssa Giacobbe, "The Complicated Sex Life of Baby Boomers," bostonglobe.com, June 25, 2014.

24. Erica Jagger, "7 Ways Sex Is Way More Awesome in My 50s Than It Was in My 20s," huffingtonpost.com, October 10, 2014.

25. Patty Brisben, "Like Fine Wine, Sex Gets Better with Age," December 1, 2012.

26. Ibid.

27. Bruce Lee, "Advice for Baby Boomers Who Gave Up Cannabis Long Ago but Want to Give It Another Chance," leafly.com, no date.

28. Ibid.

29. Robert Weisman, "Are Baby Boomers Ready to Give Marijuana a Second Chance?," bostonglobe.com, April 13, 2014.

30. Yagana Shah, "Marijuana Use on the Rise among Baby Boomers," huffingtonpost.com, March 11, 2014.

31. "Forming Baby Boomer Band," patch.com, September 30, 2013.

32. Dennis Watkins, "The Popularity of Classic Rock, Explained!," menshealth.com, September 23, 2013.

33. Kaitlin Junod, "Baby Boomers Spend Big Bucks on Rock Memorabilia," dailyfreepress.com, April 16, 2015.

34. Greg Evans, "Magical Memorabilia Tour: Classic Rock Hits the Auction Block," newsweek.com, May 7, 2016.

35. Ibid.

CHAPTER 2. OLD DOG, NEW TRICKS

1. imbd.com.

2. Ali Durkin, "Baby Boomers Bring New Meaning to the Term Lifelong Learner," newsmedill.northwestern.edu, March 6, 2012.

3. Erin E. Arvedlund, "Philly Education Reinvigorates Baby Boomers and Seniors," philadelphiainquirer.com, April 1, 2016.

4. ceup.psu.edu.

5. newschool.edu.

6. plus50.aacc.nche.edu.

7. Ibid.

8. advancedleadership.harvard.edu.

9. Ibid.

10. "Helping Baby Boomers Find a Meaningful Second Act," pbs.org, May 19, 2016.

11. advancedleadership.harvard.edu.

12. William Alexander, "The Benefits of Learning a New Language," nytimes.com, August 29, 2014.

13. Ibid.

14. Ibid.

15. Stephanie Oswald, "Want to Learn a Foreign Language?," huffingtonpost.com, March 31, 2013.

16. Paul Marshman, "Want to Enrich Your Travels? Learn a Foreign Language," travelingboomer.com, September 16, 2014.

17. Margaret Manning, "4 Power Benefits of Learning a Musical Instrument after 50," sixtyandme.com, undated.

18. Cort Smith, "The Benefits of Music for Baby Boomers," retirementoptions.com, November 12, 2013; "The Therapeutic and Health Benefits of Learning to Play an Instrument," northwestprimetime.com, January 26, 2012.

19. Daniel J. Wakin, "Reviving Musical Dreams in Middle Age," nytimes.com, February 29, 2012.

20. Ibid.

21. artistworks.com.

22. imbd.com.

23. freddiesmodernkungfu.com.

24. Lauren Harris, "Kicking the Couch: Karate Class Caters to Baby Boomers," rapidcityjournal.com, April 19, 2014.

25. dkkarateusa.com.

26. greenhillmartialarts.org.

27. Lisa Reisman, "Enter the Dragon," tricountyrecord.com, January 4, 2012.

28. "Martial Arts Classes for Seniors," advancemartialartsconnect .com, undated.

29. "Boomers Staying Active, Being Social, and Having Fun," boomer spickleball.com; "Boomers Can Get in a Pickle with Pickleball," boomercafe. com, May 10, 2015.

30. usapa.org.

31. Ibid.

32. Ibid.

33. Stephen Winbaum, "Great New Sport for Active Baby Boomers: Pickleball," retirementhomes.com, January 23, 2014; "Pickleball Becoming Favorite Sport for Many Baby Boomers," chron.com, December 16, 2013.

34. David Plechl, "In a Pickle," chinookobserver.com, September 13, 2016.

35. Greg Mellen, "Pickleball Picking Up Fans in Orange County with at Least 13 Sites to Play," ocregister.com, September 12, 2016.

36. Jeff Piorkowski, "Pickleball Is a Local Growth Sport," cleveland .com, September 12, 2016.

CHAPTER 3. REBOOT

1. Chris Farrell, "The Rise of Unretirement," losangelestimes.com, October 13, 2014.

2. Mark Miller, "Why 'Unretirement' Might Be Your Best Retirement Strategy," reuters.com, August 28, 2014.

3. Gina Horkey, "5 Tips for Boomers Transitioning into a Second Career," aboutlife.com, November 4, 2015.

4. Philip Moeller, "Baby Boomers Find Second Careers with Encore U," money.usnews.com, August 26, 2013.

5. Encore.org.

6. AARP.org.

7. Robert McGavey, "Baby Boomers Embrace Online Dating: How's That for a Retirement Plan?," thestreet.com, March 13, 2016.

8. Lucy Bayly, "Golden Oldies: One in 10 Americans Dating Online Is a Baby Boomer," nbcnews.com, February 11, 2016.

9. Jennifer Wright, "Older Singles Are Getting Frisky on 'Tinder for Seniors,'" newyorkpost.com, January 24, 2015.

10. Quentin Fottrell, "What Baby Boomers Can Teach Millennials about Online Dating," marketwatch.com, February 11, 2016.

11. stitch.net.

12. stitch.net.

13. Nancy Keates, "Hip, Urban, Middle-Aged," wsj.com, August 13, 2013.

14. Sandra Block, "10 Great College Towns to Retire to," kiplinger.com, July 2014.

15. Ibid.

16. Ibid.

17. Sarah Mahoney, "The Rise and Fall of the Fitness Generation," aarp.org, April/May 2014.

18. Ibid.

19. Anne Dimon, "Wellness Travel: 10 Trends for 2014 and Beyond," traveltowellness.com, October 24, 2013.

20. EVENHotels.com.

21. Janice Lloyd, "Aging Expert Vern Bengtson: Boomers Will Return to Church," religionnews.com, November 22, 2013.

22. Ibid.

23. Roger Sands, "5 Underrated Self-Discovery Trip Ideas," usnews.com, January 1, 2016.

24. Sarah Gold, "Nine Great Meditation Retreats to Find Your Inner Zen," travelandleisure.com, undated.

25. Ibid.

26. Chopra.com.

CHAPTER 4. INNER MUSE

1. Nedra Rhone, "Art Gallery with Atlanta Roots Helps Baby Boomers Find Success in Second Acts," talktown.blogmyajc.com, July 8, 2016.

2. Lloyd I. Sederer, "The Best News for Baby Boomers in a Long Time," huffingtonpost.com, November 16, 2013.

3. Brent Green, *Marketing to Leading-Edge Baby Boomers: Perceptions, Principles, Practices, Predictions* (Ithaca, NY: Paramount Market Publishing), 134–135.

4. getkathysmith.wordpress.com.

5. creativeaging.org.

6. Ibid.

7. Ibid.

8. Ibid.

9. Jennifer Forker, "Start a New Career? These Baby Boomers Did," Associated Press, June 4, 2013.

10. Ibid.

11. Ibid.

12. boomerinas.com.

13. Ibid.

14. Ibid.

15. huffingtonpost.com.

16. boomercafe.com.

17. nextavenue.org.

18. elaineambrose.com.

19. betterthanieverexpected.blogspot.com.au.

20. theroamingboomers.com.

21. Jane Robinson, "Baby Boomers Are the New Creative Entrepreneur," moxymarketplace.com, September 16, 2013.

22. Ibid.

23. "Baby Boomers Fuel Wave of Entrepreneurship," Associated Press, December 20, 2013.

24. Ibid.

25. aarp.org.

26. Annie Pilon, "Spotlight: Bizstarters Helps Entrepreneurs over 50 Build Businesses," smallbiztrends.com, August 10, 2016.

27. Claire Sully, "The Volunteer Revolution—What Makes Baby Boomers Such Good Volunteers for Arts, Charities, and Museums?," linkedin.com, March 30, 2016.

28. Ibid.

29. americansforthearts.org.

30. artsandbusinessphila.org.

31. artsbiz-chicago.org.

32. Ellen Gamerman, "Docents Gone Wild," wsj.com, June 24, 2015.

33. Maria Di Mento, "Baby Boomers Poised to Give $8 Trillion, Study Says," philanthropy.com, October 22, 2015.

34. Ibid.

35. Julia Halperin and Javier Pes, "US Museums Capitalise on Baby Boomers' Desire to Write Big Cheques," old.theartnewspaper.com, February 19, 2015.

36. Jordan Levin, "Jorge Perez—Building a Cultural Legacy," miami herald.com, April 15, 2016.

37. Ibid.

CHAPTER 5. BUCKET LIST

1. imbd.com.

2. Shelley Emling, "23 Things on Boomers' Bucket Lists in 2015," huffingtonpost.com, December 31, 2014.

3. Ibid.

4. Nick Easen, "Bring on the Bucket List," bbc.com, April 26, 2012.

5. Ibid.

6. passportintime.com.

7. tandemskydivingschool.com.

8. grandcanyonwhitewater.com.

9. padi.com.

10. nascarracingexperience.com.

11. Jayme Moye, "10 Best Stargazing Sites in the U.S.," fodors.com, October 14, 2015.

12. Julie Zeveloff, "The 10 Most Exotic Golf Courses in the World," businessinsider.com, April 24, 2012.

13. Ibid.

14. rockcamp.com.

15. artsandculturaltravel.com.

16. cordonbleu.edu.

17. Dave Schilling, "Desert Trip," theguardian.com, May 3, 2016.

18. fulfillment.org.

19. Carrie Kahn, "As 'Voluntourism' Explodes in Popularity, Who's It Helping Most?," npr.org, July 31, 2014.

20. habitat.org.

21. Ibid.

22. 23andme.com.

23. celebrationsoflife.net.

24. zegrahm.com.

CHAPTER 6. HIGHER GROUND

1. Diana Raab, "Hunting for Wisdom: Musings of a Baby Boomer," psychologytoday.com, February 8, 2015.

2. Laura L. Carstensen, "Baby Boomers Are Isolating Themselves as They Age," time.com, May 12, 2016.

3. headspace.com.

4. hup.harvard.edu.

5. Ibid.

6. Ibid.

7. Scott Hanson, "A Baby Boomer's Four Keys to Happiness," boomercafe.com, August 14, 2016; Andrew Stark, "Getting Ready for Overtime," wsj.com, November 2, 2012; Adam Plunkett, "The Science of the Science of Happiness," newrepublic.com, March 22, 2013.

8. Bonnie Jean Teitleman, "Baby Boomers Aging Well," bu.edu, May 2015.

9. Louise Brown, "Boomers Have an Edge over Millennials in Happiness, Study Suggests," thestar.com, June 6, 2016.

10. Jeanine M. Parisi, George W. Rebok, Michelle C. Carlson, Linda P. Fried, Teresa E. Seeman, Erwin J. Tan, Elizabeth K. Tanner, and Rachel L. Piferi, "Can the Wisdom of Aging Be Activated and Make a Difference Societally?" ncbi.nim.nih.gov, September 17, 2009.

11. Jan Johnston Osburn, "Baby Boomers Rejoice! We Really Do Get Smarter with Age," projecteve.com, November 13, 2014.

12. Ibid.

13. wisdomresearch.org.

14. Ibid.

15. Saul McLeod, "Maslow's Hierarchy of Needs," simplypsychology.org, 2016.

16. Ibid.

17. Carol Anderson, "Finding Meaning: Understanding Boomers' Expectations for the Second Half of Life," practicemanagementblog.onefpa.org, June 26, 2012.

18. Leslie Hart, "The Betterment Trend: Pursuing Wellbeing," kitchenbathdesign.com, June 27, 2016.

19. Melissa Thompson, "Self-Actualization Is the New Carrot Everyone Is Chasing," newsblaze.com, July 23, 2016.

20. Ibid.

21. Matthew Brown, "Religion May Play More Prominent Role in America as Baby Boomers Age," deseretnews.com, December 29, 2012.

22. press.princeton.edu; Wade Clark Roof, *Spiritual Marketplace: Baby Boomers and the Remaking of American Religion* (Princeton, NJ: Princeton University Press, 1999), jacket copy.

23. Janice Lloyd, "Aging Expert Vern Bengtson: Boomers Will Return to Church," religionnews.com, November 22, 2013.

24. Ibid.

25. Eric Nagourney, "Why Am I Back in Church?," newyorktimes.com, October 3, 2102.

26. Ellen Frankel, "5 Reasons Jews Gravitate Toward Buddhism," huffingtonpost.com, March 26, 2013.

27. Ibid.

28. Rose Caiola, "Aging with Consciousness," huffingtonpost.com, December 11, 2015.

29. Ram Dass, *Still Here: Embracing Aging, Changing, and Dying* (New York: Riverhead, 2000), 6.

30. consciousagingalliance.org.

31. Ibid.

32. noetic.org.

33. Ibid.

34. "Baby Boomers Preoccupied with Grandchildren's Well-Being," interimhealthcare.com, November 20, 2011.

35. Richard Eisenberg, "Boomer Grandparents: Taking It to the Next Level," forbes.com, October 8, 2015.

36. Ibid.

37. Ibid.

38. Barbara Graham, "Boomer Grandparents: Are We Really Different?," grandparents.com.

39. K.C. Summers, "Grandparenting 101 for Baby Boomers," washingtonpost.com, May 7, 2015.

40. Ibid.

CHAPTER 7. BOOMERPODS

1. Lawrence R. Samuel, *Aging in America: A Cultural History* (University of Pennsylvania Press, 2017), 9, 159.

2. Ibid.

3. aarp.org.

4. Ibid.

5. agelessons.com.

6. Ibid.

7. Julie Rovner, "Boomer Housemates Have More Fun," npr.org, May 22, 2013.

8. goldengirlsnetwork.com.

9. Joseph Gallivan, "Boomers Find Peace of Mind in Shared-Living Arrangements," nypost.com, November 4, 2013.

10. Teresa Mears, "How Baby Boomers Are Creating Their Own Retirement Communities," money.usnews.com, April 20, 2015.

11. alumni.umich.edu.

12. alumni.usc.edu.

13. Brian Jewell, "New Boomer Groups Emerging," grouptravelleader.com, January 15, 2014.

14. alumni.cornell.edu.

15. harrismade.com.

16. alumni.northwestern.edu.

17. Laura McQuarrie, "Meetup's Baby Boomer Groups Organize Socialization," trendhunter.com, March 24, 2015; meetup.com.

18. meetup.com.

19. Ibid.

20. Ibid.

21. wildboomerwomen.com.

22. Lisa Nicita, "Building Social Networks Key for Baby Boomers," azcentral.com, April 12, 2104.

23. Rob Petersen, "7 Best Examples of Brand Communities," barnraisersllc.com, November 11, 2104.

24. Pat Hong, "10 Exceptional Examples of Brand Communities," linkdex.com, January 15, 2015.

25. Keith Loria, "Are Brand Communities the Future of Marketing?," econtentmag.com, April 15, 2015.

26. "7 Best Examples of Brand Communities."

27. harley-davidson.com.

28. "8 Flourishing Online Brand Communities Examples," crezeo.com, undated; kraftrecipes.com.

29. sears.com.

30. allstategoodhandsnews.com.

31. Julie VerHage, "Baby Boomers Flock to Facebook While Teens Exit En Masse," video.foxbusiness.com, January 22, 2014.

32. Julia Layton, "5 Social Networking Sites for Baby Boomers," health.howstuffworks.com.

33. boomerwomenspeak.com.

34. Ibid.

35. Dotsie Bregel, "Social Networking for Baby Boomers," babyboomer-magazine.com, March 19, 2016.

36. nabbw.com.

CHAPTER 8. GRAY POWER

1. Lawrence R. Samuel, *Aging in America: A Cultural History* (University of Pennsylvania Press, 2017), 5.

2. Ibid., 26, 45.

3. Ibid., 159.

4. Rose Caiola, "Aging with Consciousness," huffingtonpost.com, November 12, 2016.

5. "The Baby Boomers Tackle Ageism," aginginstride.enewsworks .com, December 16, 2013.

6. Ibid.

7. Mark Novak, *Issues in Aging* (New York: Routledge, 2011) 440–442; Frank Newport, Jeffrey M. Jones, and Lydia Saad, "Baby Boomers to Push U.S. Politics in the Years Ahead," gallup.com, January 23, 2014.

8. Rick Hampson, "Whether Clinton or Trump, Baby Boomers will Reclaim White House Next Year," usatoday.com, May 23, 2016.

9. Amy Zipkin, "Baby Boomers Are Finding Second Career in Politics," nytimes.com, March 25, 2016.

10. Ibid.

11. Ibid.

12. aarp.org.

13. "The Grey Market," economist.com, April 9, 2016.

14. Matthew Boyle, "Aging Boomers Stump Marketers Eyeing $15 Trillion Prize," bloomberg.com, September 17, 2013.

15. livewellcollaborative.org.

16. Sarah Steimer, "Baby Boomer Women Remain Invisible to Marketers," ama.org, September 28, 2016; Elizabeth S. Mitchell, "Why Brands Need to Stop Ignoring the 'Invisible Goldmine' of Baby Boomer Women," adweek.com, August 28, 2013.

17. "The Grey Market."

18. Ira Wolfe, "Baby Boomers Still Got Game," huffingtonpost.com, August 24, 2016.

19. Quentin Fottrell, "Boomers Won't Budge," marketwatch.com, March 8, 2015.

20. Matthew Fleischer, "Can You Blame Baby Boomers for Refusing to Retire?," latimes.com, August 5, 2014.

21. Robert McGarvey, "Why Baby Boomers Are Not Retiring," thestreet.com, February 27, 2016.

22. George Lorenzo, "Why Baby Boomers Refuse to Retire," fastcompany.com, February 2016.

23. Jamie Reno, "Baby Boomers Changing the Healthcare Landscape," huffingtonpost.com, August 9, 2016.

24. Alison Kodjak, "Baby Boomer Will Become Sicker Seniors Than Earlier Generations," npr.org, May 25, 2016.

25. Paul Barr, "Baby Boomers Will Transform Health Care as They Age," hhnmag.com, January 14, 2016.

26. "Baby Boomers Retiring in the Suburbs," nacsonline.com, June 23, 2016.

27. Barbara Eldredge, "Retiring Baby Boomers May Shift Suburban Debate on Taxes, Social Services," curbed.com, June 27, 2016.

28. Jenni Bergal, "Can Car-Centric Suburbs Adjust to Aging Baby Boomers?," pewtrusts.org, June 20, 2016.

29. Ibid.

30. Barbara Sadick, "The Graying of Suburbia," seniorplanet.org, October 9, 2013.

CHAPTER 9. PAY IT FORWARD

1. Dan Kadlec, "Redefining the 'Ideal' Retirement," business.time.com, August 29, 2013.

2. Ibid.

3. VolunteerMatch and the MetLife Foundation, "Great Expectations: Boomers and the Future of Volunteering," undated.

4. Corporation for National Community Service, "Keeping Baby Boomers Volunteering," March 2007.

5. "Keeping Baby Boomers Volunteering"; volunteermatch.org.

6. "Keeping Baby Boomers Volunteering."

7. volunteermatch.org.

8. "VolunteerMatch Recognizes Eight Companies and Organizations for Exemplary Volunteer Programs," November 4, 2016, csrwire.com.

9. MENTOR, "The Wisdom of Age: A Guide for Staff," undated.

10. mentoring.org.

11. Ibid.

12. Ibid.

13. Ibid.

14. Mary Ellen Flannery, "Survey: Number of Future Teachers Reaches All-Time Low," neatoday.org. March 15, 2016.

15. Elizabeth Olson, "Teaching as a Second, or Even Third, Career," nytimes.com, September 15, 2011.

16. Mary Ellen Flannery, "Where Are the New Teachers?," education-votes.nea.org, September 30, 2015.

17. teach.org.

18. Ibid.

19. Brandon Rigoni and Amy Adkins, "As Baby Boomers Retire, It's Time to Replenish Talent," gallup.com, January 28, 2015; Steve Trautman, "Baby Boomers & Business: The Importance of Knowledge Transfer," premierreverse.com, July 31, 2105.

20. John Boitnott, "How the Baby Boomers' Exit Will Affect the Way You Do Business," inc.com, February 9, 2016; Rex Huppke, "As Boomers Retire, Knowledge Transfer Is Key," chicagotribune.com, July 29, 2016.

21. Eric F. Frazier, "Baby Boomer Retirement: Avoid a 'Senior Moment' in Your Business," business.com, September 30, 2015; Dorothy Leonard, Walter Swap, Gavin Barton, "What's Lost When Experts Retire," hbr.org, December 2, 2014.

22. Jeff Green, "As Boomers Retire, Companies Prepare Millennials for Leadership Roles," bloomberg.com, January 21, 2016.

23. "As Boomers Retire, Companies Prepare Millennials for Leadership Roles"; Bill Shea, "As Baby Boomers Exit Workforce, Employers Don't Want Knowledge to Go with Them," crainsdetroit.com, July 3, 2015.

24. "As Boomers Retire, Companies Prepare Millennials for Leadership Roles"; David Jacobs, "Businesses Will Face a Talent Shortage as Baby Boomers Enter Retirement Age. Is Yours Ready?," businessreport.com, July 6, 2016.

25. "Too Young to Retire: A New Career Track for Baby Boomers," ipeccoaching.com.

26. "Too Young to Retire: Baby Boomers Start Coaching Businesses," ipeccoaching.com.

27. Luke Iorio, "Career Shift: Becoming a Life Coach," forbes.com, December 13, 2013.

28. Kimberli Lewis, "Why Baby Boomers Make Great Executive Coaches," linkedin.com, August 23, 2015.

29. Andrew Neitlich, "A Perfect Career for Recent Retirees and Baby Boomers," centerforexecutivecoaching.com.

30. Ann Brenoff, "'Too Old to Adopt'? Not the Case for These Parents," huffingtonpost.com, July 3, 2012.

31. Carrie Healey, "Baby Boomers Tout Virtues of Adopting at Older Age," thegrio.com, May 31, 2013.

32. Phyllis Korkki, "Filling Up an Empty Nest," nytimes.com, May 14, 2013.

33. Ibid.

34. "Older Parent Adoption," adoption.com, April 15, 2014.

35. Kim Willis, "Think You Can't Adopt Children Later in Life? Think Again: I Adopted Two Children and I'm Over 50," high50.com, November 20, 2014.

CHAPTER 10. FOOTPRINTS IN THE SAND

1. Nicole McGougan, "Survey Says! Boomers Dominate Charitable Giving," trust.guidestar.org, August 15, 2013.

2. Allison Pond, "Baby Boomers Are about to Give $8 Trillion to Charity, but They Won't Just Write a Check," deseretnews.com, March 2, 2016.

3. Patrick Sullivan, "Baby Boomers Are Foundation of U.S. Giving," thenonprofittimes.com, August 8, 2013; Jonathan Guyton, "How Baby Boomers Will Change Philanthropy," blogs.wsj.com, March 28, 2016.

4. Maria Di Mento, "Baby Boomers Poised to Give $8 Trillion, Study Says," philanthropy.com, October 22, 2015; Dan Kadlec, "Why Charitable Giving Just Hit Another Record High," time.com, June 14, 2016; Kerry Hannon, "Retiree Giving Becomes a Force of Philanthropy," nytimes .com, November 1, 2015; Merrill Lynch, "Giving in Retirement: America's Longevity Bonus," 2015.

5. Eric Nagourney, "Why Am I a Challenge for Charities?," nytimes .com, January 12, 2013.

6. Deborah L. Jacobs, "Charitable Giving: Baby Boomers Donate More, Study Shows," forbes.com, August 8, 2013; Robert F. Sharpe, Jr., "The Emergence of Blended Gifts: Are Boomers Finally Booming?," sharpenet.com, October 6, 2016.

7. "CLA Workshop, Baby Boomer Breakthrough: The New Fundraising Model," masterworks.com, March 28, 2016.

8. "Survey Says! Boomers Dominate Charitable Giving"; "Baby Boomers Are Foundation of U.S. Giving."

9. Mark Hrywna, "Donor-Advised Funds Nearing Double Digits," thenonprofittimes.com, November 15, 2016; Leon Neyfakh, "Donor-Advised Funds: Where Charity Goes to Wait," bostonglobe.com, December 1, 2013.

10. Eileen R. Heisman, "NPT Releases Our 2016 Donor-Advised Fund Report," nptrust.org, November 15, 2016; Darla Mercado, "Donor-Advised Funds Can Be Great if You Know the Rules," cnbc.com, December 12, 2016.

11. Carol Wolf, "Donor Advised Funds for Baby Boomers," jewish-cleveland.org, May 4, 2016.

12. Beth Healy, "Fidelity Charitable Now Ranks as the Top Nonprofit Fund-Raiser in the US," bostonglobe.com, October 27, 2016.

13. fidelitycharitable.com.

14. Jackie Jacobs, "Boomers Driving Endowment Growth," linkedin.com, November 10, 2016.

15. Ibid.

16. Lisa Adkins, "Gifts to Endowments Support a Strong, Vibrant Jewish Community," jewishlexington.org, August 2, 2016.

17. Sherri Welch, "Exit Strategy: More Nonprofits, Donors Turn to Endowments for Lasting Impact," crainsdetroit.com, November 3, 2013.

18. Ibid.

19. Julie Seger, "What Forever Funding Means for National Parks," nationalparks.org, July 8, 2016.

20. "Private Foundation," investopedia.com, undated.

21. Kelly Greene, "Small-Fry Family Foundations," wsj.com, March 28, 2014.

22. Shoshanna Delventhal, "Baby Boomer Philanthropy Shifts Wealth Adviser Focus," investopedia.com, October 7, 2015; Kerry Hannon, "Family Foundations Let Affluent Leave a Legacy," nytimes.com, February 10, 2014.

23. "Family Foundations Let Affluent Leave a Legacy."

24. Ibid.

25. Veronica Dagher, "Family Foundations Can Inspire the Next Generation," marketwatch.com, April 14, 2015.

26. "Baby Boomer Philanthropy Shifts Wealth Adviser Focus."

27. Jennifer Woods, "Doing Well While Doing Good: Socially Responsible Investing," cnbc.com, September 24, 2015.

28. Kevin Mahn, "The Changing Face of Socially Responsible Investing," forbes.com, April 26, 2016.

29. Scott Stanley, "Socially Responsible Investing: Aligning Investments and Values," linkedin.com, January 14, 2016.

30. Steve Vernon, "Maybe You, Too, Should Consider 'ESG' Investing," cbsnews.com, June 10, 2015.

31. unpri.org.

32. createthegood.org.

33. Ibid.

34. Ibid.

35. helpageusa.org.

36. peacecorps.gov.

37. unv.org.

CONCLUSION

1. Larry Samuel, *Rich: The Rise & Fall of American Wealth Culture* (New York: AMACOM, 2009), 264–265.

Selected Bibliography

Brown, Mary and Carol Orsborn. *BOOM: Marketing to the Ultimate Power Consumer—The Baby-Boomer Woman*. New York: AMA-COM, 2006.

Dychtwald, Ken and Daniel J. Kadlec. *A New Purpose: Redefining Money, Family, Work, Retirement, and Success*. New York: William Morrow, 2010.

Furlong, Mary. *Turning Silver into Gold: How to Profit in the New Boomer Marketplace*. Upper Saddle River, NJ: FT Press, 2007.

Green, Brent. *Marketing to Leading-Edge Baby Boomers: Perceptions, Principles, Practices & Predictions*. Ithaca, NY: Paramount Market Publishing, 2006.

Howard, Steve. *Boomer Selling: Helping the Wealthiest Generation in History Own Your Premium Products and Services*. Phoenix, AZ: ACTion Press, 2009.

Hubbell, Peter B. *Getting Better with Age: Improving Marketing in the Age of Aging*. New York: LID Publishing, 2014.

Hubbell, Peter B. *The Old Rush: Marketing for Gold in the Age of Aging*. New York: LID Publishing, 2014.

Kennedy, Dan S. *No B.S. Guide to Marketing to Leading Edge Boomers & Seniors*. Irvine, CA: Entrepreneur Press, 2012.

Levinson, Jay and Kristi A. Carter. *Guerrilla Marketing to Baby Boomers*. Seattle, WA: CreateSpace, 2013.

Reily, Stephen and Carol Orsborn. *Vibrant Nation: What Boomer Women 50+ Know, Think, Do and Buy*. Louisville, KY: Vibrant Nation, 2010.

Thornhill, Matt and John Martin. *Boomer Consumer: Ten New Rules for Marketing to America's Largest, Wealthiest and Most Influential Group.* Great Falls, VA: LINX Corp., 2007.

Weigelt, David and Jonathan Boehman. *Dot Boom: Marketing to Baby Boomers through Meaningful Online Engagement.* Great Falls, VA: LINX Corp., 2009.

Wolfe, David B. Wolfe and Robert Snyder. *Ageless Marketing: Strategies for Reaching the Hearts and Minds of the New Customer Majority.* Wokingham, UK: Kaplan Business, 2003.

Index

About the Author

Lawrence R. Samuel, PhD, is founder of Boomers 3.0, a consultancy dedicated to helping organizations create meaningful relationships with baby boomers in their third act of life. Called "the Margaret Mead of plutocrats" by Slate.com, Samuel has been a leading culture consultant to Fortune 500 companies and major advertising agencies since 1990. As one of the top-trend consultants in the country, he advised the Who's Who of Fortune 500 companies and blue-chip ad agencies across a wide variety of industries and categories. A baby boomer himself, Samuel is a blogger for *Psychology Today*. He is the author of many books, including *The Future Ain't What It Used to Be: The 40 Cultural Trends Transforming Your Job, Your Life, Your World* and *Rich: The Rise and Fall of American Wealth Culture*. He holds a doctorate in American studies from the University of Minnesota.